This book is humbly dedicated to
Urgyen Drodul Trinley Dorje,
the XVIIth Karmapa

Diamond Mind

Diamond Mind

A PSYCHOLOGY *of* MEDITATION

ROB NAIRN

SHAMBHALA
Boston & London
2001

Shambhala Publications, Inc.
Horticultural Hall
300 Massachusetts Avenue
Boston, Massachusetts 02115
www.shambhala.com

Published by arrangement with Kairon Press,
P. O. Box 100, Kalk Bay, South Africa.

9 8 7 6 5 4 3 2 1

First Paperback Edition

Printed in the United States of America

∞ This edition is printed on acid-free paper that meets the
American National Standards Institute Z39.48 Standard.

Distributed in the United States by Random House, Inc.,
and in Canada by Random House of Canada Ltd

Library of Congress
Cataloging-in-Publication Data
Nairn, Rob.
Diamond mind: a psychology of meditation/Rob Nairn.
p.   cm.
ISBN 1-57062-536-0 (cloth)
ISBN 1-57062-763-0 (pbk.)
1. Meditation—Buddhism.   2. Buddhism—Psychology.   I. Title.
BQ5612.N35   1999   99-23691
294.3—dc21   CIP

The vajra is the symbol for the enlightened mind,
which is like a diamond, indestructible and invincible,
    open and fearless.
Vajrayana is the Diamond Way.

Contents

Contents   xi

Foreword

I am very pleased that Rob Nairn has been able to write and compile *Diamond Mind*, thereby making the precious meditation methods of the Kagyu lineage of Tibetan Buddhism more accessible to students in the West. As Rob's retreat master during a four-year retreat, I am confident in his ability to put into words his experience and practice of these techniques with knowledge, skill, and clarity.

I pray that this book will help dispel the ignorance that is at the root of suffering. May it benefit all beings.

The Venerable Lama Yeshe Losal
Abbot and Retreat Master of Samye Ling

Preface

This book is based on a meditation course I presented at the Samye Dzong Buddhist center in Johannesburg, South Africa, in the summer of 1997. The course was afterwards conceptualized in book format by Brad Hammond. Whereas my first book, *What Is Meditation?*, was written as a basic guide to Buddhist principles, *Diamond Mind* explores more thoroughly—though in a personal and informal style—the issues that Western meditators in particular are likely to encounter.

Why this book? Because meditation is simple in principle but very difficult in practice. Lama Yeshe, my retreat master during my four-year retreat at Samye Ling, says it is the most difficult thing in the world to do. If it were easier more people would hang in there and become enlightened. When I showed the cover proof to Lama Yeshe he laughed. "Diamond Mind," said he. "Very hard to crack." Not quite the angle I had been thinking of, but very true.

The difficulty is that we meditators project all our unresolved psychology into our meditation and mix it up with our conditioning. So our goals, hopes, longings, expectations, and assumptions about life snag and flow into any unconscious material that arises during meditation, and cause derailment of our practice.

The other route of derailment is subtle suppression. Some minds have the capacity to use mindfulness training as a means of keeping thoughts and feelings at bay. This is suppressive. It may produce a form of calm which lasts the period of the meditation, but it does not lead to true tranquillity and certainly prevents the arising of insight.

These and other hidden reefs are subtle and not easy to spot, because much of the action happens subliminally. When I understood this I began to introduce an increasingly interactive component into my retreats. By this means I encouraged group sharing among meditators in a carefully regulated atmosphere. I have found the results to be very beneficial because meditators then recognize their own half-seen mind states in the experiences of others.

This process has proved to be very powerful in promoting the growth of penetrating insight and releasing meditators from confused, grasping cycles that they might otherwise never have recognized.

Gradually I am attempting to organize and order the material that is coming to light in this way, because I have seen how valuable it is. This book is the first presentation and it is offered with the sincere wish that it will help you, especially help you to tread the path to enlightenment a little more easily.

Dear reader, may you be happy, and generate causes for true happiness and liberation for yourself and all beings.

Rob Nairn
Tulsa, Oklahoma
15 September 1998

Diamond Mind

Introduction

Happiness, compassion, wisdom, and clarity are inherent qualities within all human beings. The true nature of the mind is gentle, peaceful, and clear. This seems difficult to believe because most of the time our minds are in a state of anxiety, agitation, desire, passion, anger, or grief—all clouds that obscure the bright, pure quality of what we truly are. We ourselves are generating these obscurations and thus keeping our innate qualities inaccessible within our minds.

Through understanding the psychology of meditation we can reverse our perspective, and recognize these obscurations, how they came about, and how to release and dissolve them. The innate brilliance of the mind then naturally manifests.

Meditation is inherently simple. We do not need to import anything new into the mind. There are no complex, intellectual mechanisms involved. We don't have to understand profound philosophical systems. What is necessary is to learn the very basic simplicity of being—and in this way discover the diamond mind.

"What is presented here is like a map; it is an entirely different experience to actually make the journey. It requires a guide to make this journey, and as well, we must make the proper preparations: our minds must be tamed and trained through the practice of meditation. Only then can we see the *vajra* world."—Chögyam Trungpa, *Journey without Goal.*

1

What Is Meditation?

One of the greatest strangers is this one in the heart

The Journey Inward

What is meditation? It is you and me, it is us! Our inner journey, our business, our effort. Nobody can do it for us. Meditation is a method of gaining access to our inner wisdom and compassion—and resolving our inner problems in the process.

Right at the beginning it is important to let go of the idea of technique because as soon as we get caught in it, the idea arises of applying some form of manipulative formula to ourselves which takes us from here to there. Normally we might think in terms of what's the technique for doing this? Or what's the technique for making that happen? When we use the "technique" word, we set our minds in the wrong direction: the direction of thinking that there is success or failure.

As soon as we are in the success/failure dimension with meditation, we're in trouble, because there is no success in the normal sense. For instance, if somebody asked if you were a successful human being, you might regard that as a rather peculiar question. I'm a human being. I may be successful in my profession or something else, but I've never asked myself the question, "Am I a successful human being?" I'm just living. I wake up in the morning, open my eyes, and I'm living. I didn't open my eyes successfully this morning, I just opened them and I didn't fall asleep successfully either, I just fell asleep. So we are just human beings and we don't need to think success/failure in order to be alive.

So, in meditation, we are not working with the success/failure paradigm at all. We are simply training ourselves to be present in the moment with exactly what is there. For most people the big surprise is that what is there is a bewildering stranger. One of the greatest strangers in the world is this one in the heart. We don't know much about ourselves.

When we start looking, we discover there is a great deal we don't want to be with, don't want to know about, don't want to feel. Meditation reveals a paradoxical situation. We are traveling through life with a stranger who at some level is trying to communicate with us, yet we want to know only a very limited aspect of that communication. We want to know only nice things about ourselves: whether we are happy, good-looking, enjoying things. If we experience anxiety, anger, guilt, depression, jealousy, and other unpleasant emotions (which we mostly know as a sinking feeling that gets pushed down into the pit of the stomach) then we definitely don't want to know.

As we go into meditation and start encountering ourselves, we start to discover things that may be surprising. Often we don't have language to describe what we discover, so it is useful to borrow from the language of psychology. It may not always be the most appropriate terminology, but it seems to be about the closest we can get. We can use those skills that our Western culture has developed to get some perspective and understanding about ourselves.

Towards a Description

To attempt a loose description rather than a definition of meditation, one could say it is a training based on mindfulness. This entails being present in the moment, which is the ground out of which tranquillity arises. One comes face-to-face with the mind and learns about it at a deep level. This leads to inner understanding and penetrating insight into the illusion we have created about ourselves and the nature of life. Hence Buddhist meditation is often loosely termed "insight meditation," which describes the result of training in mindfulness.

Mindfulness is the founding cause of both tranquillity and penetrating insight. When the mind is established in these two, we experience liberation from suffering and a co-emergent manifestation of compassion and wisdom. But the result is not the goal. We let go of goals and focus on the action of meditation. If we fixate on a goal, we block the arising of the meditative condition.

An Attitude of Acceptance

Meditation, then, involves being present with what is there. We make discoveries about what is there, and then need to develop skills for working with the unknown and unwanted areas. The skills lie not in technique but in attitude. There is a whole series of TV soap operas that feature people with "bad" attitudes and what effects they have on others. There is a very big part of each one of us that we can call bad attitude. That's why these soap characters are so popular, because they play out our own unacknowledged bad attitude.

In meditation, the bad attitude we need to know about is the attitude we have towards ourselves, the attitude of non-acceptance of self. It arises because the mind, as we will discover, is constantly performing an act of surveillance regarding itself. We understand this principle in relation to daily life where we are always checking things out around us.

For example, when we arrive at a place for the first time, the mind instinctively scans it. It has a look at the house, the garden, all the surroundings, and forms very immediate impressions and opinions about whether it likes, doesn't like, or is comfortable with what it sees. The mind does that. We don't have to tell it to. It's the same when we walk into a room for the first time. We register very definite impressions of it. I don't think we walk in with the intention of carrying out this surveillance; the mind just does it. Why? Because this is habitual; we habitually do certain things.

At an external level we are evaluating all the time, and for very good reasons. We want to know whether we like, are indifferent to, or dislike a situation. If we like it, we are prepared to remain there. If we don't like it, we want to get out as quickly as possible or change it to suit ourselves. If we can't do either of those, we become concerned with being able to ignore it as much as possible. This external surveillance is constant and serves our primary concerns: whether we like whatever is there, whether we don't like it, whether we can change it or whether we have to adopt some other strategy if we can't change it. That's how we go through the world and that is what motivates us in almost everything we do.

This external surveillance method also operates inwardly. We conduct surveillance in relation to our inner environment. We refer to this as subjective because we are a subject and it is within us. Objective is concerned with external objects. The one form of surveillance is objective and directed externally. The other is subjective and directed internally. The level and intensity of internal surveillance exceeds the external because there are no outer forces to change it.

Externally we may see somebody who initially looks quite unkind or unfriendly and we might think, "I don't like that person." Then the person smiles and does something friendly and we think, "Oh, I do like this person." Our impressions can change because of external changes. Internally, however, we pick up something about ourselves and it doesn't get a second chance. For example, we see the arising or changing of a thought, feeling, or mood and the mind snaps into judgement about it. There is no external force to change the reaction, so if the mind churns up some sort of dark, queasy feeling, we will immediately judge and react to it. The mind will then lock into reactive mode. And it can stay there a long time because we are caught in our inner or subjective energy system. There is no external force to help us out of it. This accounts for changing moods: why we feel this way sometimes, that way sometimes, why moods change unaccountably, and why we have feelings of not being able to control our inner environment. We are trapped in our inner reactivity.

When meditating we need to take account of this sensitive inner situation. Meditation first trains us to be present with what is there, with this inner environment. We need to identify the critical nature of our internal surveillance in relation to this inner environment. If we don't, we buy into the internal criticism, the repression, and the not wanting to know. This leads away from meditation into morbid introspection. Our way of observing ourselves becomes harmful because it can lead to self-rejection, repression, and paranoia instead of clarity and freedom. Then people say, "Stop dwelling on your faults and neuroses. You're always dwelling on your miseries." That's morbid introspection.

The second thing we do is train ourselves to develop an attitude towards ourselves which won't precipitate that condition. An attitude where we say, "Whatever arises is OK." Not OK in the sense that it's what we want, but that we can be with it. We don't have to try to get rid of it. Internally we cannot get rid of mind states. If anxiety arises in the mind, we can't get rid of it any more than if the liver has a problem, we can tear it out and get rid of the problem. So it's extremely important that we really understand this attitude of self-acceptance: this is me, at this moment. It doesn't mean it's always going to be me. It means it's me now and the first thing I can do as a human being is come to terms with myself, learn to accept myself, as I am. This is the first major act of compassion that I can perform towards myself as a human being.

We can use the analogy of a carpenter who is going to make something. The first thing he does is get a piece of wood. He looks at it. It may not be the wood he wanted, but it is all he could get from the local hardware shop. So he looks at it and asks, "What kind of wood is this?" If he wants to make something out of hard oak and he has a piece of soft pine, he has to change his way of operating because if he tries to make this object out of the wrong material, it's not going to work. So he says, "Ah, I've got a piece of pine. It's badly cured; it's twisted, split, cracked. Now how am I going to work with that? I can still do something with it but I may not be able to do exactly what I wanted."

This is how we approach ourselves. "What sort of human being am I? When I stand back and look at myself objectively am I a piece of hard oak, or am I this really wrecked piece of pine which didn't get properly cured and is now split and cracked from being left out in the rain?" In approaching ourselves in this way, there is no point in condemning. There is no point in saying, "How dreadful, I have a big crack down the middle." We just say OK, that's what there is to work with. It may not be what I wanted, but it is what I've got. In meditation, it means developing the attitude where we can say that whatever arises in our minds is OK.

As we do this, we'll begin to discover that nothing is permanent. Particularly with the human mind. Even though we may start off with the most crippled, wrecked, and neurotic mind, it will not remain that way if we work skillfully with it. Learning to work skillfully with the mind is our life's great work and can yield only beneficial consequences.

Beyond Ambition: No Goals

There are no goals. If we think, "I'll now develop the attitude of acceptance because then I will have an amazing mind," we have fallen into the third hole: that of forming a goal. As soon as there is a goal, there is a potential problem because it brings with it the idea of achievement or failure. We need to understand the general principle, that change will come about if we learn to work skillfully with the mind but we don't make change the goal. That's not our job. The change will arise in its way and in its own time due to the effect of meditation. Our job is to train ourselves through mindfulness, increasingly to be simply present in the moment and to come to terms with what is there. If we do that, everything else falls into place.

This is the order of things then: First, training ourselves to be present in the moment with what is there. Second, developing the attitude of self-acceptance so that whatever arises is OK, thus coming to terms with ourselves. Third, abandoning all goals.

Having no goals bewilders most people in the beginning because in life we are obsessed with goals. "How can we get anywhere if we don't have a goal?" The answer is that if we let go of the idea of getting anywhere we come to see that we are already there. There is nowhere to go. We are sitting where we need to be, but just haven't realized it. Once we've understood that, we can relax, let go of the terrible strain of striving to achieve, to get there, to accomplish, to win. We can also let go of the accompanying fear of losing and failing. Wherever there is hope there is going to be fear in this context. So having no goals, we just learn to relax, be fully with ourselves, and OK about ourselves.

Motivation: Realizing Our Inherent Potential

Why are we learning to meditate? There are many different reasons. The first may be that we are screwed up psychologically and it's painful to be like this. We want to find some way of getting free of our anxiety, stress, tension, nervousness, depression, guilt. We want to find some way of working creatively with these. That is a very simple bottom line. Within this, we realize that as human beings we have a greater potential than just living, eating, working, sleeping. Within the human being is the potential for developing a phenomenal level of wisdom, compassion, and clarity. The great beings throughout the ages have shown us that there is a potential within all of us that is much greater than we normally manifest.

When I first started reading psychology, I remember one of the things that really fascinated me was Abraham Maslow's study of peak experiences. These peak experiences just sounded so lovely. It's as if you've suddenly stepped into a new world. So I started thinking, "I want to have peak experiences," but then I realized they were very rare and seemed to require mysterious conditions to precipitate them. Next I realized that peak experience is the potential human condition. It doesn't have to be this peculiar thing that happens only now and again and then vanishes; it is the potential human condition. We can live at peak experience. However, this type of mind state is normally dealt with only within the realm of mysticism, so we tend to regard it as being of a different order, unattainable to ourselves. But it is a deeper aspect of meditation, namely the self-actualization of our inner potential. It may not happen overnight but sometime in life, we may start experiencing this. There are beings in the world who do constantly manifest it. This then becomes another aspect of why we meditate: to actualize our potential.

Within the Buddhist context, the most important motivation is the third one, compassion for others. We look at the human condition, and what we see is immense suffering. Many beings are in suffering and we may have a tremendous sense of wanting to help. When we see someone in suffering, we do want to help them, don't we? When they are utterly miserable, broken, and devastated we really want to help them. But often at this moment we encounter our inner sense of helpless inadequacy. We may find that we just don't know how to help this person, we don't know how to reach out to them, we don't know what to say or how to approach them. Maybe the best we can do is put an arm around them and tell them some dreadful lie like, "Don't worry, it's all going to be OK." We don't know what to say so we fall back on these platitudes.

We begin to understand that if we are going to be able to help others, we really need to develop certain qualities within ourselves. We need to free ourselves from a lot of our own inner confusion and turmoil. Then the inherent wisdom, compassion, and clarity start manifesting so that we will know how to help. More than knowing what to do, we will be able to do it. The wisdom will enable us to know, but if we lack compassion, we won't be able to do it. So the third motivation to meditate is to develop compassion, because we realize that there is suffering in the world and we would like to help.

These are the reasons why we meditate: so that we can develop our inner potential, and actualize our own peak experiences without making them into goals. But most of all, so that we can really equip ourselves to help other beings. Our being in the world then becomes a natural, beneficial force so that simply being is beneficial instead of harmful. Without continually thinking, "Oh, I must do good things," the way the mind is becomes beneficial. By freeing the mind from its negative and neurotic patterns and liberating our inner potential, we experience a spontaneous response which will be helpful and beneficial to others. It's not contrived. We don't have to keep thinking about it or fabricating it.

Effects of Meditation

The effect of meditation, in the beginning, will be a gradual understanding of what is meant by tranquillity, what is meant by the mind becoming tranquil. It is not something contrived or imposed or imported from outside. It is the arising of what is already within us. As the mind becomes tranquil, many things begin to become clear. Things that were not formerly clear to us about ourselves, the world around us, the way we are living, relationships. We become clear about everything. So we need to generate within our minds the conditions for a preliminary level of tranquillity to arise. This is done through training in mindfulness—the essence of meditation.

As tranquillity arises we begin gaining insight into the state of our own minds. Insight may arise naturally with tranquillity. That is the traditional teaching. We train in tranquillity and insight naturally arises.

Insight is the most profound level of learning. It is learning through direct perception which naturally gives rise to understanding. It is not learning through externally acquired information, something imported from outside. It leads to wisdom because it is learning inwardly about how we are and what we are as human beings. The way to wisdom and intelligence is to understand ourselves as human beings. Not through a theory, not through a concept, but through direct experience. Direct perception: "Ah, that's what my mind does. That's why I become angry. That's why I become depressed. That's why I become anxious." There is no theory. It's direct perception. We see, through meditation, what the mind is doing, moment by moment. Why? Because we are training ourselves to be present. If we are present, we naturally bring our intelligence to bear on the moment. Therefore we have no option but to find out what is happening.

The effect of this is that the mind inevitably changes. We don't make it change. It changes. It is like giving a child food; it eats. Through eating, its body changes. We don't get the child up in the morning and say, "Right, eat your breakfast and grow big and strong." The process of eating naturally does it. The process of meditation naturally brings about tranquillity, insight, and change. Through that change arises the basis for wisdom, compassion, and clarity.

Meditation in Practice: Guidelines

When we practice meditation, what we are doing is training the mind to live fully in the present. It is called training in mindfulness.

The average human mind is in a state of constant distraction. The distracted mind cannot experience reality because it is scattered and confused. The essence of distraction is movement away from the present. By learning to live in the moment we focus the mind and thus experience its hidden depths of wisdom and compassion. These qualities are always present but cannot be accessed within the turmoil and confusion of the distracted mind. Mindfulness is the opposite of distraction.

Mindfulness is a faculty latent in every human mind but seldom developed. It is the ground for inner tranquillity and penetrating insight into the nature of the mind.

One can describe meditation in logical steps. The continual practice of meditation causes mindfulness to grow—just as training with weights causes muscles to grow. The growth of mindfulness brings about changes within the mind—just as applying heat to a cake mix brings about change. These changes manifest in specific ways:

- The growth of tranquillity. The human mind is naturally inclined to be tranquil, just as water is naturally inclined to be still. Distraction causes turmoil within the mind. So the mind that disengages from distraction is able to experience progressive levels of tranquillity without needing to introduce anything new into its experience, or apply inner force or control. Tranquillity arises if appropriate conditions are created.

- When the mind becomes tranquil it automatically becomes clearer: like still water, the sediment settles. The meditator is then able to experience insight into the mind. This leads to direct perception about what the mind is doing and how it is doing it. Hidden psychological mechanisms, which normally operate at subliminal and unconscious levels, are revealed to conscious awareness, creating the conditions for inner healing, growth and, ultimately, direct experience of the nature of the mind.

There can therefore be a phase where meditation parallels some aspects of psychotherapy.

In traditional training, the focus is on development of mindfulness with the attendant arising of tranquillity, and then the gradual arising of insight. The meditator receives little or no direct training in the development of insight, because normally this arises naturally with the growth of tranquillity.

It seems that many Western meditators do not experience this natural arising of insight—perhaps due to the complex psychology of technological minds. The result is that people hit plateaus and don't "progress"; their minds become rigid and closed instead of open and flexible. They unwittingly use the meditation as a way of suppressing or negating psychological process instead of promoting it. Due to this, unresolved psychological states remain buried. Since these are the ground within which negative and conflicting emotions are rooted, there is no "progress" at any level. The mind becomes rigid and narrow, inner defenses are unwittingly reinforced, the meditator remains in denial about negative conditions, and the flowering of awareness and wisdom becomes impossible.

So we begin to explore and make friends with the mind, to develop an attitude of playfulness as we embark on an adventure through a series of meditation practices. They are designed as interactive exchanges between meditators and an experienced meditation helper—preferably in a group situation. But practitioners can do them alone.

The principle being worked with is that the average human mind tends to view its internal process selectively. This means it sees only what it wants to see or is comfortable with. Everything else is repressed, denied, and projected. This tendency will be strongly present in meditation. By their nature, tendencies are unseen forces within a mind that lacks insight. Since the existence of a tendency prevents the arising of insight, a circular trap is present. I have seen meditators caught in that trap for years and years. These practices are offered as the antidote.

Meditation Support

When we begin meditating, we need a reference point for the mind to prevent it getting lost in distraction. This is called a support. Breath is generally used. Sound is also a good support.

An Adventure

Try these meditation practices and see what happens. Only after you have completed one should you look up the guidelines for helpers at the back of the book. Then you can repeat it until you feel you have understood the purpose of the practice. Ideally, form a group with a few friends. Take turns being the helper, but only the helper should read the guidelines in advance.

The practices are scattered throughout the book. They are numbered to help you keep track and to refer to the guidelines for helpers at the back.

Ending Every Session

At the end of every session, run your mind over this prayer:

> May all beings have happiness and the causes of happiness.
> May they be free from suffering and the causes of suffering.
> May they know the true happiness that is sorrowless.
> May they be free from attachment to some and aversion to others and know the great impartiality of life.

PRACTICES 1 & 2

Meditation Using a Support

Sit comfortably with the back straight.

Using Breath as a Support

Rest the attention on the breath at the nostrils. Keep the attention light and relaxed. This is not concentration because you are not trying to exclude or suppress thoughts. Allow them to come and go, but gently hold the mind's focus on the breath. It's like doing a task while music plays in the background. You can hear the music but your mind remains on the task.

Soon you drift away into thought. As soon as you realize this, simply turn the mind back to the breath. Don't do anything to the thought, like trying to push it away or suppress it.

Every time the mind drifts, repeat this. Never try to hold the mind rigidly or forcefully on the support. Keep it relaxed in its focus—almost casual. Make the act of returning to breath gentle—don't wrench the mind back.

Using Sound as a Support

The principle is the same as with breath. Here you focus on sound. Do not create special sounds like music. Allow whatever sound is present around you to provide the focus— sound of traffic, wind, voices, whatever.

The focus of the mind is open and receptive so you allow sound to come to you. Don't go hunting for sound. Try not to seek out specific or preferred sounds. Whatever is there will do. Allow whatever sound predominates to command your attention and rest with it.

When your mind drifts, gently return to sound in the same way as you did when using breath.

Meditating with a support is the basic training in mindfulness. You always do it for developing mindfulness and tranquillity.

Practice 1: Switching Focus

Meditate on the support. Allow yourself a session of 15 or 20 minutes.

Three times during the session deliberately switch your focus from the support to whatever thought is arising at that moment. Make the thought your support for 20 or 30 seconds. Then return to the normal support.

Observe what effect this has on the mind. It will clarify your understanding of how to work with the support.

Practice 2: Abandoning Focus

Meditate on the support, allowing a session of 15 or 20 minutes. After 5 minutes, deliberately choose not to focus on the support or anything at all. Simply allow the mind to go free. Tell yourself you don't have to do anything.

See if you can discover how the idea of having to do something causes tension in the mind. When there is no sense of having a task to do the mind relaxes.

Learn about the relaxed state. Allow it to become the basis of your meditation.

TIME: Do each practice three times.

2

Outlook and Looking In

Everything we need is already here

Attitude

In the previous chapter, we began with the very basic principles relating to meditation. The attitude we bring to the meditation is important because it relates to the way we are dealing with our own minds, emotions, thoughts, and changing moods.

We often have great difficulty accepting ourselves. We select the parts of ourselves we want to know about and we prefer not to know about others. When we meditate, that selective process creates problems because meditation is a process of opening up totally to ourselves in all dimensions. The selectivity prevents this essential openness and is the basis of non-self-acceptance, self-hatred, insecurity. We therefore need to train ourselves to become much more accepting, much more gentle, much kinder to ourselves so that we can learn to become more present with whatever arises without generating extra problems. These problems can arise from our responses to the insights that develop through training in mindfulness.

As we have seen, tranquillity arises in the mind when we practice mindfulness. Tranquillity is not a quality which we set out to create. It's not a thing which we acquire externally and import into the mind. It is not something that we fabricate. It's a quality that already exists within us: when we create the conditions to free ourselves from the turbulence of the mind, we naturally experience tranquillity. It naturally arises.

Gradually, as we spend more time meditating, we begin to understand that all the enlightened qualities are already within us. But they are obscured by a variety of factors. That is why in the classical Buddhist literature you read about what is called the "obscurations." That's exactly why they use that term. They are mind states which obscure our experience and knowledge of the enlightened potential within us. The more we understand that, the more we can relax about ourselves because we begin to understand that everything we need is already here. Our task as meditators is to gradually create the conditions for the removal of what stands between us and the experience of the enlightened condition: the obscurations of the mind.

The obscurations are rooted in what we call mind poisons: greed, hatred, delusion, pride, and jealousy. (Lamas say that Westerners have invented a sixth: guilt.) That is why we're always concerned with identifying and freeing ourselves from these mind states. In simple terms it means facing and becoming free from negativity. The path is neither to dwell on the negative nor to deny it. It is the mature middle way of acknowledging the existence of the negative and then setting out to do something about it. The path to freedom from negativity has the development of mindfulness as its foundation.

Finding Out Where We Are

Mindfulness is a faculty which is latent in all human beings. If we understand this, it's easier to understand why and how we meditate. It's like any other faculty, such as a faculty for music or mathematics. Like these, mindfulness lies dormant until we do something about it. If we want to become musicians, we practice and gradually that faculty grows and becomes expressed.

While we tend to understand this about life, we don't understand it about meditation. As a result, many people come to meditation with a kind of mystical, magical view. "If I sit down in the right posture, wearing the right clothes, with the right expression on my face, and in the right environment, something magical should happen in my mind." This is a fallacy that so many people bring to meditation and some books perpetuate the idea. They describe this bizarre scenario of somebody coming in off the street, having led a busy chaotic life, sitting down, learning a technique, and suddenly having a profound experience. It's like expecting somebody who has never touched a musical instrument in their life, to come into a room, sit down, and play some complicated piece of Beethoven just because they have decided they wanted to be a musician. It's as unlikely as that.

So we take a practical approach to meditation. We understand that it is a steady work of cultivating and developing something which is latent. Some people have naturally developed a bit of mindfulness in their lives. Others have developed none at all. It depends on life situations. So when we decide to start meditating, we are simply beginning a very practical, ordinary, mundane activity of training ourselves to be mindful. As we train, the faculty of mindfulness begins to develop and strengthen. Just like your ability to play the piano, or do mathematics. The difference is, when you play the piano, or do mathematics, you have a way of measuring your progress. Last week I could only do the scale in C major but this week I can do it in G major as well, or whatever it is. I have progressed. My fingers are a little more skillful, my knowledge of the keyboard a little more extensive, my knowledge of music has developed, and so on. After a year I can look back and say, "Yes, when I started I plonked along, but now I can play something."

With mindfulness it is more subtle, so it's more difficult for us to know that it is developing, because it doesn't develop in the forefront of the mind. It doesn't develop in the mind that is looking with its cognitive, intellectual, analyzing, rational faculty. It develops laterally. It is a deep broadening of the mind that slowly increases sensitivity and perceptiveness. It increases one's self-awareness, the capacity to see and know and understand what's going on in one's own mind and then around oneself. This is a subtle process because sometimes we don't quite realize we have picked things up. It takes a bit of time to recognize the change.

It is also a process of steadily bringing ourselves out of distraction. Or, if we remain in distraction, beginning to know when we are distracted. Formerly, we didn't know we were distracted. Where there is no mindfulness, we are distracted, and we don't realize it. We are so into our daydreams or whatever that we walk into walls and trip over our feet. Slowly, with mindfulness, those areas are pushed back. So in terms of actual training, it's all about mindfulness. That's where all effort is directed. If we focus on training and developing mindfulness, everything else will automatically develop. If we switch on a light in a room, the darkness is dispelled and we automatically see what is there. If we develop mindfulness the ground for pro-found inner growth is prepared, and we experience deeper states of consciousness.

Mindfulness can be defined as knowing what is happening while it is happening, no matter what it is.

PRACTICE 3

Observer Consciousness and Activity Mind

The essence of meditation is training in mindfulness. This is done by resting the attention on an external meditation support, and returning it every time it drifts away into thought.

This action is possible because one part of the mind observes and identifies with thoughts and feelings as they arise. If we did not have this capacity for self-reflective awareness we would not know or realize we were thinking when thinking happens.

We call the part of the mind that observes "observer consciousness," and the part that thinks and gets observed "activity mind." When we talk of the "thought," the word includes feelings and emotions.

The Practice

Sit in a quiet place and relax.

Don't think about anything.

Almost immediately you will find yourself thinking. It's as though thoughts and feelings enter your mind of their own accord.

Spend some time simply observing this interesting fact—that thoughts arise, so that "you are thinking," but at the same time a part of you is able to observe the fact that you are thinking—almost like an outsider watching something happening.

Carry on doing this until you become familiar with these two parts of your mind.

Next, ask yourself: Which of them is me?

TIME: Five or ten minutes a day for seven days.

Q & A

It seems there is a difference between mindfulness and the skill in learning to play the piano, in that if you haven't played the piano for some time, you can still play your scales, whereas with mindfulness, if you don't meditate for a while, it feels as though you are right back to square one?

But interestingly, the very sense of being back at square one shows that you still have mindfulness because when you started, you didn't know you were at square one. Very seldom do people get knocked right out. Mindfulness is resilient. Once you have started cultivating it, it's as though a force gets generated within the mind that is very powerful.

Another thing that can happen as you start training in mindfulness, is that if you compare your first meditation session with the tenth it often looks as though you have got worse, because by the tenth session your mind seems to be more chaotic and more distracted than at the beginning. That is a good sign because at your first session, your mindfulness was so weak that you were hardly picking up on any of the distraction or waywardness of the mind. One moment of being tranquil seemed something amazing. Progressively, as your mindfulness develops, it reveals more and more of the chaos in the mind. So you might think it is getting worse, but you are simply beginning to see what was always there.

We have been brought up in a culture where we are taught to always ask, "What's the bottom line?" We feel we have to have an answer but it seems that through meditation we can arrive at a point where there is no bottom line. It seems that the answer is that there is no answer. It is strange to realize that, in fact, there doesn't have to be an answer.

That is a very good point. In life, the bottom line is that we must have an answer. Then, when we get to these places in meditation where there is no answer, what the mind starts saying is, "If you haven't got an answer, you've got it wrong." This is the next implication in life. If you are having an argument with somebody and you haven't got an answer, they say, "Ha! You have no answer. I'm right. You're wrong!" But in meditation we enter neutral ground, open space, and there may not be an answer or a need for one. We are in a different context. This is so valuable to learn. Then we start becoming much more flexible with ourselves.

If one spends time with Tibetan lamas, this aspect of their behavior is highly disconcerting because they will quite happily embark on the most amazing courses of action without being able to give a full reason why they are doing it. If you keep questioning, you realize that they think you are a bit silly to be so concerned about a reason. They say, "Why are you so fussed? We are just going to do this." In life, we don't do that. If we don't have a good reason then we are not allowed to do a thing. But, with the mind, it's great to do these things without reasons! What is it all telling us? That it is the rational mind that wants these reasons. And in this context, it is the rational mind that is always the focal point for egocentric grasping. As we move into this other area, we are beginning to trust the non-rational part of ourselves that is not going to keep itself in bondage to existing knowledge and rules. So we are bursting our limitations. We're going beyond them. Can we allow ourselves to sit and not know what we are doing and keep on doing it? That's how we break through barriers.

Doesn't this mean that you are no longer being mindful?
No, it doesn't mean you are not mindful. You can be very mindful of not knowing why you are doing it.

But then why would you continue doing it?
I don't know. There doesn't have to be a reason. It's like being a child. The simplicity of a child that just moves with some inner knowing.

Is that what play is?
Yes, that's why play is important. This is really getting to areas where we realize how over-serious we are about life. How we become so deadly boring because everything has to be serious and secured in advance. And insured. It's so stifling. So we play. That's definitely disconcerting for overly controlled and controlling people. They don't like to see adults play—especially if the play is a bit inane.

Is there any difference between the use of the words: mindfulness, awareness, and wakefulness?
Yes.
Mindfulness is the systematic training in knowing what is happening, while it is happening. So if I'm standing here waving my right arm around, if I'm mindful, I know I'm doing it. If I'm not mindful, only you know I'm doing it. Mindfulness is this moment-to-moment precision about your consciousness in relation to your body, mind, and environment.

Awareness is a quality of knowing which develops out of that. A quality that involves becoming more panoramic in your encompassing of whatever is happening around you without directing your attention specifically to it. If I become mindful, I become more aware of things both within and without. So awareness develops out of mindfulness.

Wakefulness is a term that is used in a number of different contexts. In Buddhism, the term wakefulness is applied to that quality of mind which is no longer slumbering in distraction. It is a mind which is no longer lost in not wanting to know. It is a quality of mind that is spontaneously present and alert and therefore picking up what's going on. So it is a sharpening of awareness. It is also applied to somebody who has woken to the true nature of his or her own mind in which case it has a much more extended meaning. That means that you are beginning to move into the area where you are enlightened. The Buddha was often referred to as the Awakened One. Awakened to all the illusions and freed from them. The analogy that is often used is that the non-enlightened state is like being asleep. This is because your Buddha-nature, your enlightened awareness, is masked by the sleep of ignorance, greed, and hatred. When you awake to the fact that that is all part of the illusion of egocentricity, you are free from that illusion. So you are awakened from the ego-illusion and all that goes with it.

These three terms are useful to look at because they describe the different stages we experience. It's quite useful to see meditation as a growth process, rather than a mystical or magical experience. As a growth process, it has its own systematic order. It's graduated. Within the Kagyu* lineage of Tibetan

---

* The Kagyu is one of the four main traditions in Tibetan Buddhism. The Karmapa is head of this lineage.

Buddhism, they talk a lot about the graduated path to awakening because it's a path where we are trained to find out where we are now. To start from where we are and then learn how to move forward from there. This may sound pretty obvious, but many paths don't do this. They don't suggest that we find out where we are and come to terms with that. Instead they present us with all sorts of transcendental panoramas and create an expectation in the mind that we should be able to leap straight away to some very exalted condition. This is catastrophic for inexperienced meditators who then find themselves attempting things which are impossible. They lose confidence, lose their whole impetus. So it is very important to understand that it is a graduated path and, inevitably, we are somewhere along it. The skillful thing is to find out where we are. Maybe that means finding out that we are very distracted and lacking in mindfulness and awareness. We may find that we are very heavily loaded with egocentric grasping and negativity. That's fine. We all have to start somewhere so we start there. But at least we are now able to move forward in a practical and realistic way.

Beyond Expectations and Assumptions

So we start with mindfulness. Mindfulness is knowing what is happening, while it is happening. When meditating, it's useful to remember that little definition, "Knowing what is happening while it is happening," and we can add, "no matter what it is," because subtly we will ride into meditation with expectations. We will have a subtle expectation that when we meditate, the mind should somehow suddenly become peaceful or something like that. So if a disturbing emotion arises in the mind, it says, "Now I have gone wrong. Now I have lost mindfulness." But if we remember that definition we realize that if we are aware of the arising of a disturbing emotion, we are still mindful. We are still meditating. So it does not matter what mind state arises, or if peace, tranquillity, or bliss arises. It doesn't matter if pain arises. Or if anxiety arises. It doesn't matter if anger arises. Whatever arises is perfectly OK, provided we know it when it happens.

Sometimes, when we are meditating a lot, the mind feels so pulverized, we don't know what's going on anymore. We don't know whether we are meditating or not, whether we are awake or asleep. It usually comes after lunch. Often we sit there and think, "What is happening? Am I meditating?" If this happens, simply ask, "Do I know what is happening, while it is happening? Yes, I know. I'm experiencing a real brain-smash! My mind has gone out of focus. I can't come into focus . . . Can hardly keep awake . . . Don't know whether I'm following the breath or sound. But at least I know it, so I am still mindful." So it's very, very simple. I know what is happening, while it is happening, no matter what it is.

This frees us from all the assumptions that meditation should produce specific experiences or states. We are able to relax, no matter what is there. We can relax with anything that is coming up in the mind because we know that we are still mindful. There will be times when the mind becomes heavily distracted and we can't do anything about it. So we just watch the distraction. In this situation we won't be fully mindful— just partially. It's as though there is a spectrum with total mindfulness at one end and total distraction at the other. We are usually somewhere between the two.

When we are training in mindfulness, we can observe our own distraction. So, what this approach does, is help us understand that mindfulness is this amazingly versatile, flexible quality which is not dependent upon the arising and changing of different mind states, moods, thought patterns, and so on. It is something in itself—the ability, the power of knowing or observing.

There is a legal term that describes it very well. Mindfulness is *sui generis*. It is its own origin. It is self-arising, from its own source, not dependent upon anything else within the mind. So mindfulness is not dependent on how we feel or what we are thinking but upon its own inner strength. That is what we are cultivating. As we cultivate mindfulness, a totally new quality arises within the mind. Mindfulness produces what seems like a new mind. It is not a mind that suddenly washes out everything that was there before and produces something new and sparkling. It is a mind that slowly changes like the dawn. The dawn changes night to day. Mindfulness changes bondage, ignorance, and the other mind poisons to enlightenment.

This is why in some books on meditation we read phrases like, "It does it." This is because the quality and energy of mindfulness does what has to be done. The conscious mind does not have to rearrange our mental environment. We don't have to bring in new things, or change things. It is done through mindfulness. That is also why over and over again we hear meditation teachers using phrases like, "Let it be. Allow it. Let go." In the beginning, we don't understand those phrases. We think our conscious mind has to do it. We have this overdeveloped sense of responsibility. "I must do it. I must make it happen." But all that mind has to do is bring us into the room, sit us down on a cushion, and bring us to our meditation support. That is the extent of that mind's responsibility. Then it all happens. But very few of us can carry that one through. Because that same mind is also concerned with a lot of other factors that prevent us from even getting into the room. That is the biggest difficulty: getting ourselves into the room or place of meditation, wherever it is.

The Four Foundations of Mindfulness

The foundations are four points that we can refer to for strengthening our mindfulness. Although we are using an external meditation support, we can now add four points to them: body, feelings, mind and its states, and mental contents.

1. *Mindfulness of the body.* The body can become a help to mindfulness. Check the body at the beginning of the session and now and again during the session. What is happening in the body? Do we know? The body is resting on the ground; we can feel the weight of it, the contact and sensations within the body. We can know a lot about the body, because it is continually affecting our mind states. The body is not separate from meditation. If the body is comfortable, relaxed, and at ease, the mind will feel more relaxed. That is why it is essential to be comfortable. If the body is not comfortable, the mind will start becoming tight and tense. Then we will think we can't meditate. So this is the first foundation.

2. *Mindfulness of feelings.* This is difficult to distinguish from the third foundation, which is mindfulness of the mind and its states. This refers, first, to the sort of feelings that ripple throughout the body, but that aren't completely physical. Flustered feelings going through the nervous system, fluttering in the stomach, running through the veins. They relate to the impact of emotion on the body. So check those out.

Then, what am I feeling emotionally? Am I happy, sad, excited—or is the emotional tone calm and neutral, with no discernable emotion arising? Amazingly, many people are out of touch with their emotions and don't know what they are feeling. They don't know what emotions are present because they may be in denial about theirs. This can cause havoc within the mind. If I am in denial about my emotions, there is no possibility that my mind will become tranquil. There is no possibility of the mind settling, because the suppression and denial of these emotional states create continual underground turmoil. It is like a revolution that is being suppressed. It is always going on behind closed doors. There is always a hidden element which encourages dissent and this inevitably becomes public and creates tension. So find out what we are feeling, learn to be OK about our feelings. Acknowledge that feelings are happening.

3. *Mindfulness of the mind and its states.* This means, what sort of thought patterns, what sort of mood am I in? For example, I could be in a state of clarity or very dull. Or there could be a mix of mind and emotion that produces states like anxiety, a mind/feeling state. Depression too. Or unease. There is a whole range of different conditions which form a background to everything else. They set the mood. What is the mood? What is my overall mind state? Curiously enough, these change of their own accord. Sometimes in relation to external events, sometimes in relation to body chemistry, sometimes in relation to what we have eaten, or as a result of a movement within the unconscious. Moods change. So we check those out and get to know them all as they come and go.

While we are meditating, every now and again, we can

check those. In doing so we begin to discover that our mindfulness can be clarified simply by knowing that there are separate areas from which it is affected within the overall movement of the psyche.

4. *Mindfulness of mental contents.* The fourth foundation usually relates to our overall picture of the world or our philosophy of life. Taking Buddhist examples, we study certain teachings which liberate the mind, for example, the teachings on impermanence. As we study those teachings, they have an impact on the mind. That impact will, now and again, arise in the mind spontaneously. We may be doing something that is causing us a problem in life and then suddenly this realization of impermanence arises and we realize, "Ah, I don't have to get all stewed up about this. It's not a big deal." So we are much freer in the way we work with things. That's why we often reflect on topics like impermanence, precious human birth, and karma: they help the mind free itself from the bondage of grasping. When those states arise in the mind, they arise with a potentially liberating content. So we become aware of mental contents.

Conversely, mental contents may lead us to bondage. We may find the mind has negative patterns or beliefs, ideas, and projections that we are not fully aware of. If they arise and we dwell on them, act them out, or in some other way feed energy into them, they increase the state of bondage.

We train in the four foundations, and refer progressively to these in our meditation without making a big deal of them. Just being aware of these different aspects. When meditating, we check them. We may think, "I'm having a very disturbed meditation today, what's going on?" Then realize, "Ah, I've got indigestion. The state of my body is affecting my mind and that's why I feel like this." So we realize that the body does affect the whole situation. Then we may have tremendous clarity and think, "Why did this happen?" Then realize: mental contents. A sense of freedom arose because suddenly we realized something about impermanence. In doing so, we let go of everything, and the mind just cleared because we realized we didn't have to make a big deal of it. These changes come about all the time in relation to one or more of the four foundations.

Not only do we train in the simple method of returning all the time to our meditation support, but we start training systematically in giving ourselves these other supports, the four foundations.

3

Hidden Reefs

Recognizing the intricacy of our mind patterns

So far we have covered a few basic areas such as why we meditate, what meditation is, and the motivation for meditating. In the first chapter, we looked at the method and the effect of meditating and I focused quite a bit on the importance of being clear about the attitude we bring to the meditation and the importance of learning to accept ourselves and come to terms with what is there. I made the point that meditation isn't technique because if we get into the mind-set of thinking of it in that way then we expect to achieve results and to have success, and then we fear failure.

Another problem arises if we work with technique: we work with something which is manipulating the mind, whereas the purpose of meditation is to release the grasping action of the mind so that the inherently enlightened qualities can manifest. That can't be done through the application of a technique. All technique does is rearrange the existing mind patterns. Although it is not difficult to understand the method in meditation, it is difficult to understand what we need to bring to it in terms of attitude. The basis of that is complete openness. An open acceptance of ourselves the way we are.

That's easy to say and we hear it a lot in life but what it means is recognizing the intricacy of our mind patterns. The extent to which we are continually judging and evaluating the contents of our own inner environment. How the thoughts, the feelings, the sensations, the moods, whatever they are that arise and pass within the mind, are under continual surveillance. That surveillance is there because we want to check out that inner environment and know whether it's what we want or what we don't want. If it is what we want, we grasp it. We try and hold it. For example, if a mood, or a mind state arises that we like, we want that to stay. We want to be like that all the time. And the mind says, "This is how it should be." So we try and grasp that state but the very act of grasping destroys it. So the joyful clarity of the mind, which is inherent within the non-grasping mind is continually lost through the egocentric grasping action.

Conversely, if mind states arise which we don't like, we try and push them out. We want to get rid of them. We don't want to feel them. We don't want to know them. So repression, suppression, projection, denial, all those psychological mechanisms come into play. These are the means by which we keep ourselves in a continual state of unrest, tension, and dissatisfaction. While those non-accepting mind states are present, the mind cannot rest because it is in conflict with itself all the time. If a thought or a feeling arises that we don't like, then we try and push it out. We then not only have the negative emotional state, but we have the conflict of trying to be rid of it. If, in meditation, we are not aware of this—which most people aren't—instead of meditating, what we will do is engage in a semi-conscious unseen war against our own mind states. We'll try and use the meditation as a means of continually avoiding what we don't want to be with and continually trying to nudge thoughts and feelings out of the mind that we don't like.

What that will produce, in the initial stages, is tension. A sense of not achieving or of failing. A sense of struggle. If it goes on a bit longer it produces a rigid mind. If it still goes on after that it produces a paranoid mind. So our meditation goes into reverse. We aren't meditating; we're just tightening the bolts. Making the mind tighter and tighter.

This is why it is so important to look at this issue of attitude right at the outset. We say to ourselves, "This is it. This is what I have to work with. Let's find out about it. Let's be clear about it and come to terms with it. A full, unqualified acceptance of the way I am."

We are told that what a growing infant needs most is unconditional love. If we develop this attitude of acceptance, we develop unconditional love towards ourselves. We let go of all the conditions where we accept ourselves if this, or we don't accept ourselves if that. This then is the basis of compassion. Acceptance produces an extremely resilient mind because inwardly the mind is relaxed and OK about itself. Then whatever arises in the way of thought or emotion can be accepted and worked with comfortably without fear or reactivity. That is why the first issue we always focus on is our attitude.

Motivation, then, is the next big important thing. Within the Buddhist system, the fundamental motivation is to transform our own minds in order to be able to help others. That is the primary concern. If we can sort out our own minds and develop the inner qualities, then we will be able to help others. Although meditation is often seen as a selfish activity, because we are continually working with ourselves, it is the most altruistic thing we can do. This is because, what is within the mind is what we will express in the environment around us. If our mind is loaded with secretly oppressed negativity, that is what we will inevitably express in the environment around us. There is no option. If, however, we learn to come to terms with all the negativity and learn to transform it, then what will automatically be projected into the environment will be love, compassion, clarity, and wisdom.

The basis of meditation, then, is the method of mindfulness. Bringing the mind into the moment. The first consequence of training in mindfulness will be tranquillity, when the mind begins to settle while being released from the causes of inner turbulence. In Sanskrit, tranquillity is called *samatha*. Out of the tranquillity arises the capacity to see what is really going on within the mind and this is called penetrating insight. The Sanskrit word is *vipassana*. This is where the mind, through its clarity which comes about due to tranquillity, develops its inherent power to see and know and understand exactly what is happening within it. Through this we begin to gain true understanding about ourselves.

The big distinction between meditation and learning is that meditation leads to wisdom and compassion because there is a process of true understanding through direct experience and observation of our own mind states. Learning is acquiring information and adding it to the mind. Learning will never penetrate to the depth of meditation because it is simply acquiring new concepts. The more we meditate, the more we realize that concepts are superficial. They only have to do with the rational, conscious, logical, intellectual mind. There is a very definite point in meditation where we have to let go of all that. So it's a case of moving from fixation on the conceptual, rational mind and learning to move inward and trust ourselves and our own instinctive understanding that arises through insight and self-perception.

Expectations

Within attitude is expectation. We are very seldom aware of our expectations. They are part of the background to the way we are. For example, if we go to a movie which has had a good write-up, we go with a certain sense of excitement. We are going to see a good movie. As we walk into the cinema, we don't say to ourselves, "I have an expectation that this is going to be a good movie and I'm going to enjoy it." The mind doesn't do that, but it carries the message unconsciously. The result is that if the movie isn't very good, we will be disappointed. If it's only half reasonable, we say, "That wasn't really so great." What has happened is that the mind has gone in with a very high expectation. It set a high standard and if that high standard isn't met, there is disappointment. It may still be a good movie, but it hasn't met that high standard. So experience is determined by expectation.

Conversely, if somebody said, "That's the most useless movie ever made," and we can't get in to any other movie house so we go and see it and it is half reasonable, we enjoy it because we went in thinking, "This is going to be a load of junk." So we are pleasantly surprised and enjoy it. Once again, our level of enjoyment is determined by our level of expectation.

The third scenario is where we have no expectation at all. In this case, our minds are open. We receive the experience with a freshness, alertness, and quality of intelligence that is not there if there is expectation. Whatever happens has a vividness and interest of its own because we are not judging it against any criteria. We are looking at it as it is and allowing it to be itself. With meditation this is crucial. We may go to meditation with an expectation that it is going to solve all of life's problems, that if we sit for ten minutes, all our emotional issues are going to dissolve, or if we sit for twenty minutes we are going to become totally blissed out. Some people walk into the meditation room with this sort of expectation. They are so locked into their expectation that they sit down and put a fatuous smile on their faces because somewhere their mind is saying, "If I pretend that I'm being blissed out then maybe I will be. Or perhaps I should be feeling blissed out because it seems as though everyone else is and if I pretend that I am that way too, then maybe I can get in on the act." This is a very painful thing to do to oneself because it's not true. Pretending isn't going to make any difference to the normal flow of one's mind states. They are going to continue as they ever did. So if we go to meditation with this sort of expectation, we are going to run into a brick wall and it is going to be painful.

Then we probably think, "If I meditate for half a day, I'll become enlightened." Some people believe that! Or maybe they think a weekend will get them enlightened. Once again, it doesn't happen, so there is great disappointment. The curious thing is we don't realize the connection between the expectation and the consequence. Therefore when the effect that we have expected hasn't arisen, all sorts of reactions come into place. Either we dismiss the meditation as something that doesn't work, or we decide, "It doesn't work for me. There is something especially wrong with me that makes meditation impossible for me." Very often, people get the impression when they are meditating that everybody else around them is doing fine. They look out of the corners of their eyes and think,

"These other guys are really cool. They've got it together. They are doing what's expected and I'm the only one who's getting it wrong. What's wrong with me?" That, of course, destroys confidence. Very soon one gives up.

So we can see expectation is one of the most fundamental obstacles to meditation. When we start meditating we come across the term "obstacles" over and over again. It's as though we have gone for a drive. We thought we were going to drive along a beautiful motorway. After about half a kilometer there is a landslide, we can't go any further. That is an obstacle. Until we understand the nature of the obstacle and what to do about it, we can't go any further: we always stop there. And it is exactly the same with expectation. Until we understand the existence, the nature, and the effect of it, we will always stop there. We will run up against it but we won't know what has stopped us. We'll just know we've hit something.

We start to become aware of our expectations and we train ourselves to pick up on them. This is not easy because they are buried at a semi-conscious level, part unconscious and part subliminal. It is a belief system we bring into the room with us. So we really need to reflect on what our expectations are.

Assumptions

Assumptions are quite similar to expectations. Due to our expectations we assume certain things. We assume meditation is going to produce certain effects. We assume we are capable or incapable of certain things. However, assumptions blind the mind. They make us incapable of seeing what is there. They are the basis from which we misinterpret experience and external data. For example, if we walk into a room of strangers and somebody frowns at us, we'll immediately think, "That person doesn't like me." We've made our assumption. What we didn't know was that at the moment we walked into the room that person had a really bad stomachache and was frowning because of the pain. However, until something happens to dispel that assumption in our mind, we believe we "know" that person doesn't like us. We are doing this constantly in our lives. It is a fundamental aspect of the way our minds are working in relation to the world and people around us.

When we meditate we inevitably make assumptions about what we should be able to do. One assumption we may make is that we should be able to "clear the mind," because we have read this dreadful phrase in books. We also assume that we are going to be able to get rid of our thoughts and negative mind states because we have also read this in books. So we believe that when we sit down to meditate, we should somehow be able to click the mind into a different realm. If that doesn't happen, we feel that something has gone wrong. You won't believe the number of times I've said to groups of people, "When you meditate you cannot clear your mind, you cannot stop thoughts, you cannot get rid of emotions," and within ten minutes of the first exercise somebody will say, "When I started meditating, I couldn't get rid of these thoughts that kept coming back to me."

When we are locked into our assumptions we do not hear or see. Information bounces off and goes into cyberspace and never comes back! It cannot penetrate the assumptions. We have to find out about our assumptions because they cause us to become completely deaf and blind.

Goals

Next comes goal orientation. This is the assumption or expectation that in our meditation we should be achieving
something. Goal orientation is one of the hidden reefs upon
which meditation founders. It is a submerged mental factor—
we don't see it. We hit it and it rips the guts out of our meditation.

Goal orientation contains a number of factors within it. First,
it's a mental concept. A goal has to be conceived by the thinking mind. The thinking mind is not the one that meditates, so
when we lock into it we cannot go beyond the concept. Thus
meditation is blocked and we simply sit waiting to achieve the
goal—but we never get anywhere. We can remain stuck like
this for years.

Second, it contains within it all the potential for stress. As
soon as we have a goal, all our conditioning relating to achievement comes into effect. It clicks in with our entire psychological history. It clicks in with all the goals we have attempted to
achieve throughout our lives, and all the straining, stress, tension, and pressure that have gone into trying to achieve those
goals. So too all the fear of failure, and actual failure, humilia-
tion, and stress that have gone with that; the rare moments of
achievement that we fear we will not be able to repeat. All those
and many others come in with that one thing and they lodge in
the mind. So the mind drags into the room an immense amount
of unresolved self-torment. We sit down and torment ourselves.
We think, "Now I have to meditate, I've got to achieve a goal."
The result is self-torment, striving, and no meditation.

If we have understood that we do not have to believe our
expectations and assumptions, then the ground upon which
our goals are usually built is removed. This is a dismaying expe-

rience for the goal-oriented mind because now it asks, "What should I expect? What should I focus on? What should I try and achieve?" Then comes the worst bit of advice for the driven mind: "Nothing."

"How can I sit down and do something without a goal? This is not possible or intelligent. It's not part of the way I have been trained." But actually it is essential for meditation. To let go of the idea of linear progress across a plain from one place to another. There is no goal. We might think we can't have a journey without a goal but we can because the journey is away from the goal-oriented mind; it is into another dimension of ourselves. This isn't a mythological situation, although it can be expressed more accurately through myth. It is an actual reality for the meditator.

We cannot move toward a goal in meditation because a goal can only be defined by thought. If we ever feel we are moving toward a goal, we are simply rearranging our existing knowledge and experience. Meditation takes us beyond that. It takes us beyond concept. So how do we do this?

We let go of any sense of anywhere to go, or of any person to go anywhere. In the beginning, these may be only words. In practice we simply bring the mind back into its moment of awareness. That's all there is to do and we don't do it with any sense of a reason. We don't say to ourselves, "Now I'm doing this because of that." If there were a reason at all, it would be to side-step reason itself.

We are just doing it like a child playing with mud. It doesn't play with mud for any reason, but it is totally absorbed, fully fascinated, absolutely enjoying it. If we were to ask the child why it is doing that, it wouldn't be able to tell us. It's just doing it. This is meditation. You are simply bringing the mind back into the moment. The moment the mind is locked onto a goal, that goal abruptly ends meditation. It then simply becomes an inner struggle to achieve something.

Even though we might understand the concept of avoiding goal-oriented meditation, we may continue to meditate with goals in mind. We may still meditate with an underlying sense that now we should be trying to achieve something. As a result, the mind will do something to try and give itself a sense of achievement. It might, for example, think "I need to perfect my posture." So we study every aspect of posture and get into the most perfect posture and are so uptight as a result, that after about ten minutes we are ready to explode. This is evidence of goal orientation. Or we might think we have to do something perfectly because most of us somewhere in our minds have got this message that mummy and daddy will love me only if I can be perfect. Or, the world will only admire and accept me if I can be perfect. And that message will most certainly come up in meditation.

"I can't get my posture perfect, because I've got sore knees and a wrecked back, so now what else am I going to do to be perfect? I'm going to try and make my thoughts perfect or the way they come and go perfect. Or I'll try and make my mindfulness or my breathing perfect." So the mind starts subtly trying to control one of those. Once again the meditation gets derailed.

We have to look out for telltale signs that we are doing this, because goals are surreptitious. They sneak in undercover. They are part of our unconscious conditioning process.

Here are some of the signs that ambition is present. If we are starting to get tense, that is usually a sign that we are striving for a goal. If there is any sense of striving, there is a goal. If there is any sense of frustration in our meditation, there is a goal. Feelings of stress and irritation, particularly if there is irritation because somebody makes a noise, are both signs of underlying goals. Irritation because something is happening in the environment is a sign of goal orientation. Because the mind says, "In order to achieve my optimum meditation I have to have a quiet place; anyone who walks into the room must sit properly, they must be very quiet; dogs mustn't bark, people mustn't make noises outside." There are people who tyrannize their households. "When so-and-so is meditating, we all have to creep around the house and not make a noise." That is because we assume that in our meditation we have somehow to set up this terribly sensitive, fragile thing. Any slight interference from outside shatters it. That is not meditation, it's just trying to achieve goals and it becomes very egocentric.

If there is any feeling of not achieving, feeling discouraged or a sense of not getting anywhere, or an intensification of our favourite feeling of guilt, then those are all signs that goals are there. They have come in under our little craft and are threatening to breach it.

Letting Go of Goals

In order to let go of goals, we have to get some glimmering of the fact that they are there. We do that by saying to ourselves when we start the meditation: "It doesn't matter. Whatever comes up is OK." Most of all, see what happens to the mind if we say "I'm a failure. I'm going to fail at my meditation." See what the mind does if we do that to it. There is a sense of all this invested effort and all this accumulation that we have done over the last ten, fifteen, twenty years gone to waste. "I've wasted all that effort and I have failed." If that starts any form of reaction in our mind, we will know that it has hit the goal-oriented obsession, the hidden reef.

If somebody says to us, "You are a failure" and we receive that bit of information joyfully, then we are not working in the presence of a goal. Because to be a failure is perfectly fine and in fact at a certain level necessary. Why? All these things I have talked about are related to the conscious, rational mind and its way of being. Meditation does not happen within that mind. Meditation does not happen in the mind that thinks logically and works rationally. Nor in the intellectual, concept-forming mind. One of the difficult lessons we have to learn is that that mind has only one function and that is to bring us into this room and get us onto the meditation cushion and bring our mind back to the external meditation support. When that job has been done, that mind is finished with. It has no more to do.

After that, a different dimension of mind starts to come into operation. Meditation is multidimensional. We *get* meditated. And the only way we can get meditated is if that mind gets itself out of the way. It is like a parent that takes its child to school and then has to get out of the way. If the parents hang around at school and go into the classroom with the child, they are not only a nuisance but also an embarrassment to the child and to the teacher.

This is what we keep doing. We keep trying to take this rational mind into the meditation. It doesn't work. That is why expectations, assumptions, and goals are lethal: because they are all the subversive methods that the rational mind uses to keep itself in the picture. But the meditation picture is something else. It will reveal itself in its own way, in its own time as mindfulness develops. When we really learn this, there is an enormous relief. It is the relief of no longer attempting the impossible. No longer struggling to achieve and having the fear of failure. We can finally relax and be fully at ease. This is why accomplished meditators are very relaxed. Things don't bother them because they just let them happen. There is a kind of spaciousness about them because this tight, grasping, goal-

oriented mind has relaxed. Then we are comfortable with paradox and the apparent chaos of this creative process of mindfulness revealing itself. There is always an element of chaos
when this happens because normally we have got everything so
tightly organized and buttoned up that we think that that is the
way it has to be.

When we start meditating and moving into this other dimension, this neat and tidy buttoned-upness can no longer function. It keeps falling apart. The basis on which we build it keeps
disintegrating. There is a sense that things aren't happening the
way they "should," the way we want them to, the way we
expected them to. Always something else happens. And that's
exactly how it needs to be if meditation is to happen.

With goals and expectations, there is always a sense of being
driven. As soon as we try and sit down and relax, something
winds up inside us and says, "You should be doing something."
So we are driven to activity. When we let go of our goals, there
is an amazing relief of realizing, "I am no longer being driven."
A very easy sense of "I'll do what I can but I'm not driven to it
anymore" comes into the mind. There is no more frenetic, fran-
tic scrabbling to get there. The mind just moves along in a wonderfully open, gentle way and that anxious, driven quality
falls away.

Q & A

*Where do we accommodate the fact that we reasonably expect
things to happen in life on the one hand, and the fact that, psychologically, expectation is an obstacle to meditation?*

It's actually very easy. If you realize that you have expectations, which you do realize if you work with meditation, then

you simply accept that fact and relax with it. The reef is now seen, so you won't hit it. The problem comes when the expectation is not seen and we have locked into it.

There are two scenarios. One is: I come to a course or open a book with expectations because I've paid money and I've read the course outline and I'm not fully aware of the existence of my expectations or, more importantly, the degree to which I've locked into them. I have made it the only basis upon which I am prepared to be here. That is a very rigid mind. What happens to that mind is that if it gets here and things don't work out according to its expectations, it's disappointed, fed up, and angry.

The second scenario: the meditator's mind says, "I'll go to this course. I've read a bit about it. I know I have an expectation but at the same time I'm prepared to release that expectation and go with the flow." So I arrive and there is some crazy person there who is supposed to be giving a course. My expectation of having a nice, orderly, structured course is now out the window but I say, "OK, I'll see what this guy can teach me. It's not what I expected but I'll see what happens." I relax and I suddenly realize that this person is teaching at a totally different level. This person is teaching by violating my expectations so that I have no option but to face them, see the effect of them, and let them go. It depends on the level of our awareness and the degree to which we are caught in expectations.

There are "crazy wisdom" schools where teachers do the most outrageous things. By doing outrageous things, teachers confront students with all their assumptions and expectations and they just hit the wall. When an accomplished teacher does something crazy, there is no more debate, so the mind that tries to keep its territory through reason and grasping is simply shattered or runs away.

4

The Butterfly Mind

We are continually strengthening the tendency
of the mind to be unsettled

Why Is the Mind Unsettled?

First we need to ask why it is necessary to settle the mind, and what is the unsettled mind. Mostly, it is the mind we have always lived with, the one that can't remain on the cushion. It can't remain in this room or anywhere near this place most of the time. We sit down, focus on the external meditation support, and we form an intention. Our intention is to remain present with the meditation support.

Then a very interesting thing happens. Something within us, within seconds, perhaps within a split second, overrides that intention. In an instant, we are no longer with the meditation support, instead we are thinking about something. Now that is quite interesting if we sit back and look at it.

Here we are, these "self-deterministic" human beings who are supposedly able to guide our destinies through the universe, but we can't even carry out an intention to keep the mind in one place for more than a few seconds at best! Something else overrides that intention and we are away.

What overrides that intention? Habit. What sort of habit? The habit of having a butterfly mind. An unsettled mind. A mind that prefers to be in constant movement and activity. When we try to meditate we discover how distracted and unsettled our minds really are. It's usually quite a healthy shock to new meditators.

So our mind zaps away, out of this room. We could be in Trafalgar Square, New York, or down at a Cape Town beach within an instant of starting our meditation. Quite possibly it takes a little bit of time before we catch up with it and bring it back into this room. Then it's gone again! Then we catch up with it and bring it back into this room.

So that is the unsettled mind. It is the mind that, of its own accord, moves away. When our mindfulness is weak we don't even realize that it has moved. It's as though we fell asleep. We sit there and think, "Ah, now I'm going to meditate . . . I wonder what we will have for supper tonight?" We're gone! Now we realize that if we don't learn to settle the mind we are unlikely even to begin meditating.

How We Keep the Mind Unsettled

Interestingly, what we don't understand is that we are continually strengthening the tendency of the mind to be unsettled, and we are doing it in a variety of ways.

One is, we continually seek entertainment. It may be through TV, radio, a book, a conversation, or drinking coffee. If we are denied all those external forms, all we have left to fall back on is the entertainment of the mind's imaginative activity.

And that is limitless! It can run videos forever! It does it because we want it to. At a certain level, we most certainly want it to. It's boring and tiresome just to be here watching the breath. So we definitely want to be doing something else.

Quite often we won't let our minds settle because we are afraid that if we do manage to switch off the eternal video we will uncover what we have spent so much of our lives burying and keeping hidden. What we don't realize is that our intention to remain present and mindful is actually overridden by *another* intention which doesn't reveal itself. It is another of those surreptitious hidden reefs. That intention comes into action the moment the mind spots the possibility of doing something more interesting than meditating. So if we are using sound as the meditation support and the sounds are entertaining, like music, or strong, like the sound of an airplane, then we can really get off on that. Or if it is something nice like a bird, we can get off on that. If it is the wind in the trees we can stay with that pretty well—but after a while there isn't much juice left in these external possibilities. So our minds grow bored and feel the need for entertainment. This gives rise to a predisposition to seek distraction, so that when a thought or feeling arises, the mind is automatically inclined to engage it. If our mindfulness is weak, the engaging will happen before we realize it, and we will be into distraction. This is one of the ways we unsettle ourselves.

Unsettling through Reactivity

Then there are more rigorous ways of unsettling the mind. We start meditating and go through maybe five or ten minutes of being quite diligent in bringing our minds back to the focus.

Then, deep down, a memory stirs of something somebody said to us some weeks ago. We had an argument, which perhaps we lost. We didn't like that, so there is quite a strong residual emotional element left. This surfaces somewhere in the back of our minds and sends a tremor through the whole body. Perhaps a feeling that we didn't like this unresolved blow to our pride, or whatever it was.

Now a new thing happens. We hook into that memory and rerun it. We rerun it with all its emotional impact and this does more than the bland entertainment cycle we've just talked about. This really gets us stewed up because we completely invoke all that old business, it hooks onto a whole lot of other related emotion in our minds and before we know it, there is a good old turmoil going on. So there is no tranquillity in our meditation. We've managed to get our minds pretty turbulent. Now we're steamed up! We're ready to go and punch somebody. This is frustrating because here we are sitting meditating and nobody has even picked a fight with us, and we're ready to go and punch somebody. What have we done? Thoroughly unsettled our minds.

What we begin to see is that there are these sorts of mechanisms in operation. Although they are relatively superficial within the meditation context, they are going on in our daily lives. So if, in meditation, we spot our unsettlers, we can begin to identify them in life. We begin to see how continually throughout the day we are unsettling our minds through our reactivity.

When we are driving a car, for example, and somebody speeds, suddenly appearing over a hill and nearly crashing into us, we get a big fright. Then we get angry. Then we go through a really big scene in our mind about how other people shouldn't drive so fast and go through red traffic lights. Then

SHAMBHALA PUBLICATIONS, INC.

Mailing List
P.O. Box 308, Back Bay Annex
Boston, Massachusetts   02117

If you wish to receive a copy of the latest Shambhala Publications catalogue of books and to be placed on our mailing list, please send us this card, or e-mail us at: info@shambhala.com

PLEASE PRINT

Book in which this card was found

_____

NAME

_____

ADDRESS

_____

CITY & STATE

_____

ZIP OR POSTAL CODE   COUNTRY
                                      (if outside U.S.A.)

_____

E-MAIL ADDRESS

_____

somebody pulls in front of us, changing lanes quickly. Now we are even more angry! The piece of road in front of us, that space there, belongs to us. They should know that! They shouldn't get into it quickly, or at least without asking our permission. So by the time we get to work we are really not in a fit state to do much except growl at people.

If we go back over this whole business in the traffic, we begin to see that it is a self-generated turmoil. It is just an indulgence in reactivity. And there are very definite alternatives. The moment we got into the traffic, and the other guy was speeding, we could see what we were doing. We could know that, "OK, this is actually what happens in traffic. I do it myself sometimes. When I am in a hurry, I speed up over hills and I go through red traffic lights." I'll bet most of us have done that! So that person isn't doing anything different from what we have all done. It is just our ego territorial compulsion that is making us buy into reactivity.

If we see this we can actually let it go. If the guy pulls in front of us, we just slow down and let him go. If he wants to change lanes, we just slow down and let him go. Slowly, it's no big deal. The stress of driving through traffic falls away and we are just adjusting to and accommodating the needs of other human beings.

What we see from this example is that through our reactivity and our projection we're keeping our minds unsettled and we are convinced that it is the fault of other people. The traffic example is easy to deal with because it is so obvious, but this is going on in many areas of our lives. We are doing this constantly because we are not aware of our expectations, assumptions, and reactivity. We have probably done this so consistently through our lives that we no longer realize we are doing it.

We may say, "If only I could go away to a really nice, quiet holiday spot, I would be much more at ease. Then I would be much more peaceful and happy." Unfortunately, we wouldn't because we take with us our built-in tendency to unsettle and stress ourselves out. What we have to learn is that if we begin to understand how we unsettle ourselves, we can actually free ourselves and relax wherever we are. Not always, but pretty well anywhere. The point is that each time we unsettle the mind we strengthen the tendency for it to be unsettled. This means it will remain unsettled for a long time after the specific incident is past. In addition, because the strong tendency is there, it will unsettle itself of its own accord, even when we don't want it to. We can't blame it because we set the causes in motion ourselves.

How to Settle the Mind

It is important that we come to our meditation understanding that we are inherently inclined to unsettle our minds. External things do not generally unsettle our minds, internal things do. We are responsible for this inner environment. So we sit and meditate and then see the first unsettling action. The mind is wanting to take off somewhere. Now comes the important moment. The normal tendency is to grab the mind and wrench it back, an act of violence similar to a parent in a supermarket with little Annie, who wants to take stuff off one of the display stands. The tired, overwrought, frustrated father grabs hold of her and yanks her back. Of course, straight away there is a scream and a scuffle and a fight.

That is what happens to our mind if we treat it that way. If we wrench the mind back from its preferred course of activity we are going to create inner turmoil, adding stress, tension, and resentment to our unsettledness. We will feel an internal resistance building up in the mind. So don't attempt to settle the mind forcefully—it won't work. Try to be the kind parent: return to the meditation support gently, kindly. That's the first principle of settling—know there is no need to chase off after any thought, but when the tendency to do so arrives, simply turn gently away from the temptation and return to the support.

PRACTICE 4

Where Does My Mind Go?

Training in mindfulness entails continually returning the mind to the meditation support—breath, sound, physical sensation, or a visual object.

This exercise is concerned with the mind's avenues of distraction. The mind seems to depart from the meditation support, sometimes within seconds of being placed there. In the beginning, meditators have no idea why it moves away or that it moves consistently in the same directions. The first step in learning about the mind is to find out where it goes.

The Practice

1. Meditate normally using sound or breath as the support. Allow yourself a session of at least 20 minutes.
2. During the last 10 minutes of the session begin in a very casual, relaxed way to note where your mind goes when it seeks distraction. You can rely on memory or use a note pad.

    Do not use this as a way of punishing or disciplining the mind.

If you find that you keep tugging the mind back before it goes far, or that your surveillance is so intense that the mind "seizes up," then you are trying too hard. Your effort is getting in the way and preventing the normal flow of activity. Relax, take a break, and begin again in a more casual, relaxed way.

3. At the end of your session, look back and see what pattern is emerging.

Categorize the places your mind goes to. See how many categories you can create and identify the main ones.

TIME: Do this exercise once in a session, taking no more than 10 minutes for step 2.

Continue for one week, or until you are quite clear about your mind's normal routes of distraction. If, after two weeks, you are still not clear, don't worry.

Move on to the next exercise and you will find that this one will clarify itself in time.

Making Friends with the Mind

Sometimes, with the really strong, unsettling movements we will find that our mind does not want to come back. It is too strongly fascinated by its area of preoccupation. It slips back before we have even got it onto the meditation support.

What we do in this situation is learn to make friends with the mind. We both sit down at the negotiating table and look at our respective agendas. The agenda of the part of the mind that thinks it wants to meditate is that it wants to be mindful and present. The agenda of the other part of the mind is that it wants to be entertaining itself at some other place, wherever it is, involving itself with its emotionality, thinking something through, planning, and so on. What we discover when we observe that other mind is that there is a lot of energy invested in its alternative preference. This is why that mind keeps going there. If we try and force it back to our meditation support we are going to create tension because the energy is too strong. So we learn to make friends.

"What's really happening? Why do you want to be there?" we ask.

"I want to be there because two weeks ago I had an argument and I was defeated. I'm feeling wounded and I have somehow got to lick that wound and get it better."

"OK, there are a couple of possibilities now. Maybe we can do that for ten minutes until you are satisfied."

"No, ten minutes isn't going to be enough. I need the rest of my life for this one."

"All right, how about we postpone it."

"Postpone it?"

"Yes, until after the session."

"No way."

"All right, maybe we can postpone it for two minutes."

"Well . . ."

Now, this may sound crazy but if we've got a strong compulsion working in the mind, it is actually accessible to this form of negotiation. We negotiate whatever deal we can with that part of the mind. Two minutes may be a great achievement because if we manage those two minutes, that whole cycle will have weakened and we won't have used violence. We won't have tried to suppress it or oppose it. We will have found a way of skillfully turning our mind away from it, and will be able to repeat the same tactic again.

Then we begin to discover something about settling the mind. Settling is an extremely simple action of slipping out of an old pattern without in any way causing waves and very quietly and simply putting ourselves on the meditation support. It is possible not to follow our habitual patterns compulsively at that very primary level. Slowly we make friends until our mind settles.

Tranquillity Is Not a Lovely Feeling

Usually in a retreat situation, it will take two or three days before the mind starts feeling content to settle. Then it will still move around but it won't be like a ping-pong ball that hits a hard surface and is gone within a split second.

Learning to make friends with our mind introduces an element of realism into the way we work with ourselves. It dispels many of our mistaken ideas about what we can do with our minds and begins to introduce us to a new, far subtler, more effective way of working creatively with our mind states. Then the mind will begin to settle.

Once the mind settles, we begin to learn a lot about it. We begin to experience tranquillity. Tranquillity is the condition where our mind has settled and is happy to be present with whatever is happening. If thoughts are arising that is OK. The mind that has a modicum of tranquillity can allow the arising and passing of thoughts. We will begin to see our reactivity, the tendency of the mind to fly at thoughts, either to grab, push away, or negate them. Tranquillity does not mean that we start feeling lovely. It doesn't mean we start feeling blissful. It doesn't mean our mind stops having thoughts.

Tranquillity means that we begin to settle down in the presence of whatever is happening. Even if there is a strong painful emotion, if our mind is completely OK with that, and is not unsettled by it, we can be tranquil and be experiencing a painful emotion. It's quite a paradox, but it's true.

Something else the settling does is that it starts removing that conflict. Emotional conflict is an area of difficulty. We fight our emotions. We have inner conflict but as we learn to be friends with our mind, that inner conflict begins to subside. When the mind settles we are present in a more real, immediate, direct way with whatever emotions are there.

Q & A

I find that the moment I claim painful feelings in the body, like my ingrown toenail, as mine, I go off into a dream of thinking about it, or planning what to do about it. It seems to run its own course, and as soon as I have named it I get caught up in what I have named.

What you have identified is that you can be meditating, there can be clarity, the mind can be settled in the sense that your mindfulness is strong enough to remain more or less present and the normal activity of the mind arises and passes without you engaging it in a particular way. Then pain might arise, you focus on it and immediately you say "my pain." As soon as you have said this, you've bought into one of your means of unsettling the mind. The mind has grasped. That is the mechanism whereby the mind grasps. As soon as there is the sense of me and mine, then there is suffering, all the reactive action comes into play, and you feel you have to do something about it. Because now you're really suffering. So then you go into one or other form of distraction to get away from it.

At a certain level, the mind knows exactly what it is up to. It's just up to us, meditating with the observer mind, to be present with it. And see the humor of it as well.

Is the deeper purpose of the unsettling mind simply to keep the mind unsettled or is it genuinely attempting to work things out?

The unsettled nature of the mind is usually reactive and seeking distraction. It is the mind that wants entertainment, to pick at sores, whatever it is. It is the playing out of habit.

But does it believe that it will achieve satisfaction by keeping itself unsettled?

At a certain level it probably does believe that, but don't expect it to be a rational situation you are looking at. Most of these mechanisms are not rational. Most reactive behavior lacks rationality because it is rooted in causes that are long forgotten.

Whenever you get into reactive behavior, it's drawing on old, forgotten, unresolved issues. Therefore it will always bring more into the moment than is appropriate. Road rage is a good example. Somebody in Los Angeles was driving along in a traffic jam when a stranger behind him hooted at him. He stopped his car, got out, and shot him dead. Now that's a reactive mind! I would say that that is a reaction that exceeds the needs of the moment. So obviously that stimulus hooked into a huge amount of unresolved psychological material. That is what we are all doing a lot of the time. Whenever we are reactive, the immediate stimulus is activating a lot of unresolved stuff. That is why it is so unsettling in the mind. It's like emptying a whole lot of rubbish bins out. Suddenly there is all this chaos going on.

5

It Just Flows By . . .

Thoughts, in themselves, have no power

Stabilizing the Mind

We may think our minds are stable because we are not insane. In our culture, people who are insane are said to have unstable minds, but actually, all our minds are unstable. They are unstable in the sense that powerful mental and emotional states can overwhelm us when they arise, and throw the mind off balance. That's instability—the fact that we are susceptible to being thrown off balance.

Within the meditation context, this is how we measure instability. It doesn't mean we are insane, it means we are subject to the power of our reactive mental and emotional states before which we are usually helpless. Therefore we find ourselves experiencing extremes which we would prefer not to. Sometimes when they get us in their grip, they lead us to behave in uncharacteristic or irrational ways. What that means in daily experience is that normally we think we're fairly emotionally even. We get a little bit angry sometimes, or we get a little frightened, perhaps jealous, or happy, whatever it is.

Now and again, however, one of the emotional states becomes predominant. For instance, something might happen which makes us very angry, and then anger arises very powerfully within the mind, becoming a predominant force. We are now extremely angry and our normal mind state is overwhelmed by this. We look angry. There are sparks coming out of our eyes and angry words coming out of our mouths. That's not a stable condition! We are overwhelmed. Off balance. Because of this we do and say things that we wouldn't normally—our behavior is uncharacteristic.

Imagine a tray of water. If it's kept level, the water is level. If we tip it, all the water goes to one side. It's an interesting phenomenon. The more it tips, the more water goes there, so the more it's going to tip. The more unbalanced and unstable we get, the more we get carried by that momentum. Until eventually all the water sloshes against the side and a wave comes back to the other side and we topple back into some sort of a balance. That's how many of us go through life. Stumbling and staggering between different extremes of emotional reactivity.

If we stand back and look at that, what is interesting is even though we don't want to experience these extremes, they still come upon us. What that tells us is that the powerful patterning within the mind has the capacity to overwhelm our normal intentions or desires to be one way or another. That is the unstable mind. It is one of the biggest problems we have to work with in the world.

We know now that the unstable mind is carried by habitual patterning. We know that it is also carried by compulsive energies within the mind. Once these energies start being triggered, we get caught in compulsive cycles. If this mind state goes on long enough and seizes an unresolved emotional issue that is strong enough, it becomes obsessive. We not only get thrown over, but we experience the spiral that goes in on itself and won't stop whirling.

Changing Habitual Patterns

Why do we get toppled by these habitual tendencies even when we may know about them?

The basic cause lies in our way of being: habitual patterns of grasping and identifying with our inner contents. We create our sense of identity out of all our thoughts and feelings. We say, "I am this kind of person." So our sense of self, our idea of our identity, is attached to the way our emotions and thoughts manifest. We give that out as our identity to ourselves and others. What that reveals is that we've glued ourselves to those mind states, none of which are permanent. They are all changing, like shadows flickering across a wall. But there may be three or four shadows that we particularly identify with, so we say, "That's me."

This is yet another habit. It is a habit that causes us to grab onto and glue ourselves to these arising and passing states. Meditation helps us discover the extent to which we are continually identifying with these changing patterns within the mind. Most of the mechanisms involved are not conscious. They are flicking up out of the unconscious.

In psychology this is known as conditioned reflex: a response which is present because of conditioning which we have had in the world, because we have done it for a long time and because intelligent thought is no longer present. It's just like a machine that clicks on as soon as the stimulus triggers it. To a large degree, we exist as a lot of conditioned reflexes. Our instability works through that. Of course there are deeper psychological factors. We may have had a heavy trauma, we may be on the edge of psychosis, we may be very neurotic, there are all those other possibilities. But at the level of our experience in meditation this is what we can see.

So first of all, in meditation, we come to terms with that fact. We don't have to go home and tell our families that we are unstable. But this is the human condition. The average mind is inherently unstable in this sense.

Now let's look at meditation in relation to the human condition of instability. We have now had some experience with meditation. We now know that something very simple is going on. We sit down, form an intention to rest the mind on the external meditation support. As we saw previously, within a fraction of a second, that intention is overridden by another intention. So the mind goes off into other areas where it seeks escape, entertainment, and so on. We see it and bring it back, it goes, we bring it back, it goes, we bring it back, it goes, we bring it back, it goes . . . That is what we call meditation practice. We have not perfected meditation, we are just practicing. So we are practitioners.

Inner Surveillance

There is a continual process of arising, manifesting, and passing. Thoughts and feelings arise, have their time of being, and pass. Then a new thought arises, has its time of being, and passes. So there is this constant process.

Now that is interesting because if you are on retreat and you come to the end of a day, when you lean back against the wall, gaze out the window, and fall half asleep and reflect, you'll think, "How interesting! All that has happened is thoughts and feelings have arisen, manifested, and passed. And yet, I've had a sense all day of something very real, substantial, important, and significant going on. Why is that?"

The answer lies with that part of the mind which conducts inner surveillance. It observes every thought that arises because it has very specific requirements. It wants to have only pleasant thoughts and feelings. It definitely doesn't want to have uncomfortable, painful, or nasty thoughts and feelings and it is determined to ignore anything that is boring.

That's the agenda of the surveillance system. Out of this comes a very intense reactivity which has bound up within it a kind of excitement. When something comes up that we like, there is a tremor: "This is it. Now it has come right." So we grab it with our minds.

When something comes up that we don't like, there is another tremor. "Now it has gone wrong." We feel the meditation has gone wrong because we haven't realized the depth of our expectations. If the mind is caught in expectation without realizing it, then any mind state arising in the meditation that doesn't accord with the expectation will be experienced as "wrong." A really common expectation is that somehow meditation should produce lovely mind states. So when something different comes up, the mind says, "Oops, gone wrong. Don't like it." And it goes into another reactive phase—anxiety, depression, tension, whatever our particular cycle may be.

When something boring comes up, which is usually when mindfulness is beginning to edge in, the mind says, "Where can I go now for a bit of entertainment? I don't want to know about this." Unfortunately, none of this comes up on a television screen in words. These are all underlying, unspoken responses going on in the mind, usually at a subliminal level. But by their very nature, these responses are causing us to get glued to what arises, because it's through these responses that we assign the semblance of reality, substance, and permanence to what's coming up all the time. That's how we get tangled in our thoughts. That's why there is a constant sense of something really important and significant happening when we are caught up with our thoughts. We don't realize that the thoughts, in themselves, have absolutely no power. We are giving them power.

There are so many books written with titles like "The Power of Thought," as though there are these magnetic things floating around in the universe that now and again slam us between the eyes and make us do things. But actually thought, in itself, is no more powerful than a shadow flickering over a wall. What gives the thought power is you. Your own mind. You feed energy into it.

All the habitual patterns within our minds have arisen in exactly that way. They are creations of our own karmic activity. We have fed energy into them over and over again so they have accumulated a momentum. When they arise, we naturally get sucked into them. But we ourselves created the momentum.

Backtracking

When we see this, we start to work with some precision with our thoughts. We introduce a series of exercises. First, we begin with backtracking. When we have drifted away and we realize we are in a thinking pattern, we pick up right there. "I'm now on the beach. Two seconds ago I was mindfully observing sound. This is interesting. How did I get here?"

So we backtrack. What thought preceded the thought of the beach? It was a thought about sunshine. What preceded that?

The thought that I was feeling hot. What preceded that? The thought that I'm wearing too much. What preceded that? I was with sound, or breath. So I was with sound and suddenly my mind thought about clothing. Or maybe it went the other way around. Maybe it thought, "I'm hot." Then it thought about sun, then the beach, then I was in the sea.

In the backtracking we see, first of all, how quickly and spontaneously the mind moves. But most importantly we get to the moment of arising. We get to that moment between being mindfully resting with the external support and then . . . gone! There is always a moment. So next we recognize the moment of arising.

PRACTICE 5
Backtracking

1. Meditate normally, using sound or breath as the support. Allow yourself a session of at least 20 minutes.
2. When you find yourself thinking a particularly strong or clear thought, stop meditating and see if you can discover where it came from. See how far you can get.
3. After doing this several times, see if you can divide the pathways your mind takes into general categories. You may find that thoughts arise within the mind via a limited number of quite specific avenues!

TIME: Do this exercise at least once in a session, spending ten minutes on the last step.

1

Thought arises
at the subliminal
level

Because the
tendency to think in
a particular way has
been reinforced,
thoughts arising out
of that tendency will
arise again and the
cycle of thinking
will be repeated
indefinitely.

5

Habit is
strengthened

MIND SCHEME 1

*Cycle of thought where
mindfulness is weak or absent*

This series of steps depicts
the reinforcing of habitual
tendencies that underlie
thought. Where mindfulness
is weak or absent, these
tendencies will continue
spontaneously to produce
thoughts, even if the person
wishes or wills otherwise,
because

1. when the mind reacts it
   reinforces the tendency;

2. by projecting or acting out,
   understanding is prevented
   and the power of the
   tendency is increased;

3. just wishing for change does
   not in itself produce change
   in the mind.

2

Subliminal scanning registers the existence of the thought

→

3

Becoming aware of thought

Subliminal reactions to the thought include:

Judging: like, dislike, or indifference;

Reacting: grasping, repressing, rejecting, negating, projecting.

These two actions reinforce:

• the tendency to judge and react in this way

• the specific thought, emotion, tendency, etc., that has arisen

This act of identifying gives the thought power over the mind—like a rider mounting and taking control of a horse.

4

Identifying with the thought as "my thought."

This leads to many consequences such as:

• acting on the thought
• dwelling on it
• developing it
• trying to oppose it

These constitute the usual moment-to-moment activity of the mind.

Where mindfulness is
strong the very moment
is seen and known.

1

┌─────────────────────┐
│   │
│   Thought   │
│   arises   │
│   │
└─────────────────────┘

Complete mindfulness at
the moment of arising
frees the mind from
involvement with thought.
Only an accomplished
meditator can do this, so
the second stage will
probably arise even within
the mindfulness.

MIND SCHEME 2

*Cycle of thought where
mindfulness is cultivated*

Mindfulness

1. breaks the compulsive
   cycle of thinking;

2. stabilizes the mind, so it is
   no longer swamped by
   negative and conflicting
   emotions;

3. develops spaciousness, a
   relaxed state in which the
   mind lets go of suffering
   and begins to open up and
   experience its true nature;

4. allows true inner peace
   and freedom from thought.
   Thoughts will continue to
   arise but will be left free to
   come and go.

4

┌─────────────────────┐
│   │
│   No identification │
│   with thought   │
│   │
└─────────────────────┘

2

Scanning, judging, reacting

- Where mindfulness is not strong, the meditator may become aware of the mind's activity at this point.
- Even where mindfulness is strong, this process may still happen due to the accumulated force of habit.

3

Tendency to identify with thought is clearly seen

This is where meditators often make their first breakthrough and realize that "I am not the thought." Now thought is allowed to flow by without being engaged. The mind is not disturbed by thoughts, habitual patterns weaken, and the mind settles and becomes peaceful.

Mind learns not to identify with thought and habitual patterns weaken.

The Moment of Arising

In order to understand the importance of this moment, refer to the two mind schemes depicting what the mind does when thoughts arise. You will see that where mindfulness is absent, the mind endlessly reacts and strengthens thought cycles. Where mindfulness is cultivated, thought cycles are weakened and then broken—leading to freedom from thought.

The moment of arising is the most interesting moment of all. It is also the most important because so many things happen in that moment. Quite a lot of them are happening subliminally and we need to know about that. Basically it's like this: the thought comes into the mind from a variety of sources. Before it has fully impacted on our conscious realization, it has gone through a number of processes at a subliminal level.

- "Thought arises": number 1 in charts 1 and 2. First subliminally, our mind has picked up the approach of the thought. We may not yet know this consciously but it has happened.
- "Subliminal scanning": number 2 in charts 1 and 2. Second it scans, "What sort of thought/feeling is this?" Rather like a guardian at a door. It checks it out.
- Third, it performs a judgment and an evaluation. Good, bad, or indifferent. Like, don't like, or don't want to know about it. On the basis of this it reacts.
- Fourth, "the thought enters consciousness": number 3 in charts 1 and 2.

That's usually when we first know about the thought. That is why when we first feel the effect of the thought, we know whether it's a nice thought, a nasty thought, or a neutral thought. If we reflect on it, we realize that this process must have happened. Otherwise we wouldn't know what sort of a thought it is, we would just be aware that it was a thought. The fact that we know its value and quality reveals that some process must have preceded its arising within the mind.

Because of this process, by the time the thought hits our conscious mind, we have already reacted to it. Once we have reacted, we're lost (number 4 in chart 1). Out of reactivity comes the imbalance. Once we have reacted, we are carried away by the reaction because it has put us under the power of the thought, we've fed our energy into the process and the thought has taken us away, because we have identified with it. This is the normal cycle of thinking and reveals why habits are so difficult to break—we are constantly reinforcing them at a subliminal level.

We sharpen our mindfulness by training ourselves, once we have practiced backtracking and are quite comfortable with it, in observing the moment of arising, and identifying these processes. When we really see them we begin to understand the mind firsthand. This is the basis of insight.

Observing the moment of arising begins to broaden the boundaries of our normal awareness. It pushes conscious awareness into previously subliminal areas. We start changing the quality of our mind state. We increase our awareness. If we are around people who have developed a lot of awareness, very interesting things happen. We notice that they are picking up things that are going on around them that we wouldn't have expected them to pick up. We may be doing something behind their back and they actually know we are doing it because their awareness is so sharpened. It's as though they can see out of the corners of their eyes. If we spend a lot of time in the bush, we develop what is called "bush eyes"—the ability to detect movement and patterns in the bush that an ordinary person would not see. Bird watchers see birds that nobody else sees because they have trained themselves to do so. It's the same thing in relation to the mind.

So we discover that a lot happens in the moment of arising. The final discovery is that the moment of getting hooked into a thought actually involves a moment of decision (between 3 and 4 in both charts). There is a moment when we decide "I'm going to latch onto this thought in one way or another." We either grasp, push it away, or negate. All three of these actions leave us stuck with the thought. Now we know where the mind gets stuck. This is where the unbalancing begins to happen. This is the moment when the mind is thrown off balance because once we get stuck to the thought, we're caught in the reactive cycle associated with it.

To give an example: somebody does something to me that I don't like. It arouses a subliminal thought/feeling response which is, "This kind of thing makes me angry, I'm now going to get angry." At a subliminal level, I buy into the response, feed energy into it, and it snags all my unresolved anger. Then all my anger that has nothing to do with this situation gets activated, and a great burst of anger explodes out of me, out of all proportion to what triggered it . . . because my mind is unbalanced. Do you see that? It all started with that one tiny moment of decision. But I didn't know I had made that decision. But we humans have free will, and this is how we exercise it!

PRACTICE 6
The Moment of Arising

1. Begin as for "Backtracking," meditating normally using sound or breath as the support for at least 20 minutes.

2. When you find yourself thinking a particularly strong or clear thought, stop meditating and backtrack until you can't go any further back. This should return you to the point when your mind was resting on the meditation support.

3. Now see if you can identify the moment the first thought arose—the one that began the chain of thinking that brought you to the strong thought that began this game. For example, you may have been focused on the meditation support one moment and then thinking of your dog the next. So in this instance "dog" is the first thought, and from it others developed.

4. The next question is, why did you suddenly think of your dog? There are specific causes that give rise to thoughts. What was the cause in this instance? When you reflect you may suddenly realize, "Oh, I heard a dog bark. That sound evoked an image of a dog, which brought my dog to mind," and so on. In this way you gain insight into the mind's activity and discover the layer of mental activity (sometimes subliminal) that lies behind specific thoughts.

The Dawn of Freedom: Dissolving Conditioning

To understand the mechanics of freeing the mind, have a look at mind scheme number 2.

When we see this, we begin to realize that we don't have to pick up on thought at the moment of arising. This is the first hint of freedom in the mind: we do not have to pick up on thought. Until this realization all our processes are compulsive. We believe we have to pick up on thoughts because they appear. Even with this realization, however, because of habit, we continue to engage. But after a while, in our meditation, we see that habit and return to the meditation support, and slowly the mind lets thought go again. A new one arises, we are compelled to pick it up, we see it, we go back to the meditation support.

Each time we return to the meditation support, we weaken the compulsive cycle and strengthen mindfulness. This is the actual nitty-gritty of why mindfulness is so powerful. We are working directly with a fundamental psychological process. We are unwittingly dissolving our conditioning processes, not cognitively, but at the level where the conditioning happened. We don't need to think, "Now I am going to undo my conditioning." It just happens.

Then one day, a moment arises when we are sitting there, perhaps feeling fully brain-smashed because we have been meditating for twelve hours, we're really tired and our mind is all over the place, and a thought arises. We see it arising and then we realize that within the observer consciousness all the reactive machinery is coming into place but we think, "Oh well, I can't be bothered."

At that moment something quite remarkable happens. The thought flows by. We don't engage it or pick up on it, it just flows by. That's as if our greatest enemy walked into the room and suddenly we weren't afraid or bothered. All the old problems didn't come up because we didn't buy into the thought. That's the first moment of what we call "freedom from thought."

Freedom from thought does not mean no thoughts. It means

that thoughts come and go freely. We don't latch onto them. An incredible brilliance comes into the mind. Accomplished meditators say that the mind becomes very vivid, clear, tremendously free, and lucid. We have this wonderful free feeling because we have experienced the nature of bondage, which is habitual, and now we have stepped free. There is no greater joy for a beginner meditator than that.

The Stabilized Mind

Once we begin to establish this as our regular mode, we are not enlightened although we may think we are. Sometimes when people have that experience they think they are enlightened because it is such a brilliant experience. Such wonderful joy and clarity arise in the mind. We usually feel very compassionate as well. So when this becomes our established experience, it doesn't matter what thought arises. We start experiencing a wonderful sense of resilience because inner states no longer matter. If a really horrific thought comes up, it just arises and passes and we observe it. If a really wonderful blissful thought arises it's quite OK. It just arises and passes. If a thoroughly boring space arises, it doesn't matter.

This is the beginning of what in the Vajrayana tradition is called "one taste." It is the true meaning of impartiality or equanimity. There are many words to describe the stabilized mind which have a rather unfortunate connotation in our language. Sometimes this state is described as indifference. Can you see what an inappropriate word "indifference" is for this? It conveys the idea of this kind of deadpan, gray disinterest. But it's the very opposite. Our mind is just so free, vibrant, vivid, and unembroiled that it is impartial to whatever arises because whatever arises no longer affects us at gut level. It just flows by. We are now free at that very rudimentary level. This freedom is brilliantly yet quietly joyous.

This is a balanced or stable mind because now there is less and less possibility of being thrown off balance. There is less possibility of being caught and carried away by the thought that is arising. That is a stable mind. When it becomes constant, the whole quality of our mind changes. It's a totally different mind from the mind we used to have. There is a radical difference between that mind and the unstable mind. It would be very difficult for that mind to go back to being unstable because now we know we don't have to buy into thoughts.

So the stable mind and freedom from attachment to thought go together. That is what we are working towards. That's the first potential for the meditator. A very simple level but a very profound experience when it happens. If we can stabilize the mind in this lifetime we can be extremely glad. We will have done something very profound.

PRACTICE 7
The Cycle of Thought

All thoughts follow a standard cycle:

- a moment of arising
- a time of enduring
- a moment of passing

We don't usually realize this because so many thoughts are coming and going that the mind is in a confused jumble and we don't see the beginning or end of anything. Another reason is that some thoughts endure for a long time or recur so frequently that we can't recall a time when they weren't there. This lack of understanding about thoughts can lead one to conclude that they are "solid"—have an enduring permanence. We need to learn directly that this is not the case.

The Practice

1. Meditate normally. After a few minutes note what you are thinking and return to your meditation. Do this twice more during your session.

    At the end of the session look back at the thoughts and realize—"they have gone." Reflect on this: to have been there and then gone, thoughts must have followed a cycle of arising, enduring, and passing. Now you understand the cycle intellectually, but haven't yet experienced it fully in the sense of "being present" with all three stages.

2. Now meditate again. Observe moments of arising. If you have done the previous exercise on this topic you should be able to spot the moment.

    Now you know about two stages in the cycle: arising and enduring.

3. Meditate again. Tune in to a particular strong thought and observe it mindfully. Note how at a certain point it is no longer there. See if you can identify the moment of passing.

    This is the most difficult of the three stages to "see," because the act of observing the presence of a thought can cause one to hold onto it. It's only when your mind relaxes into bare attention that this will be seen.

TIME: Spend at least three twenty-minute sessions on each stage.

Q & A

Is this the primary practice and then the more advanced practices come after that?

No. There is no "what comes first and what comes second." This is what we do in the totality of our training, whichever form of meditation we are doing.

It seems that as mindfulness develops, a sense of inner space develops where we talk of passing thoughts and so on, using spatial language. For instance, a feeling of anxiety seems to happen down there and to the left, or anger can seem to arise from behind me.

Well, first of all mindfulness creates the sense of spaciousness. Why? Because the normal state is that we are so intensely glued to all the thoughts and feelings around us that there is never a moment when we are not overwhelmed by some or other thought or feeling. And there isn't a moment when we aren't attributing intense reality, solidity, and importance to it. So it's like a situation where we have gone to listen to music and the music is so intense that there is never a pause between notes or bars. Many people say that the significance of music lies in the silence between each note. We usually have music where there is no silence between the notes and it becomes too much. Instead of being spacious our minds are crammed full of tense grasping.

When we start meditating, we start letting go of this intensity of involvement. Then spaces develop. There are spaces between thoughts. We become aware of the tranquillity that comes about because of that. The mind begins to become peaceful and spacious. Then that internal state reflects externally. The mind, instead of grasping at every object in the room, rests very peacefully in the spaciousness in the room.

Yes, but it's also that the objects themselves feel more like mere impressions.
What is happening is that at every level we're receiving impressions through our senses. Normally we only know about them once we have interpreted them. Through mindfulness we start getting closer to the original impact, so it's purer, more vivid, and somehow more joyful. All the labored business of naming, interpreting, reacting is slowly being released.

So is mindfulness the space in which these things exist?
Mindfulness is the quality or faculty of the mind that enables us to cut away from all the attachment and rest closer to our essence.

If I am interpreting you correctly, my identity is tied up in a series of obsessive shadows, and also with this inner surveillance system that is working beyond my ken.
I really like the way you put it. We've got this obsessive compulsive involvement with shadows. In addition, the mind is working dualistically. There is the observer consciousness, which has all these surveillance mechanisms, then there is what I call the activity mind, which is the mind that is throwing up all the thoughts and feelings. Then within that complex arise our expectations, goals, assumptions. They could be located at either level.
So through the exercises we identify our assumptions and obsessions and that gives us an early warning system. This is where we learn to live skillfully.

For instance, I know there are certain compulsive areas within my mind that are still very strong and I know what sparks them off. So I do my best to avoid those situations. Not because I don't want to resolve them but I know that when those situations arise, I can't handle them. It gets too much for me. So I would rather resolve things in other areas first. Then I will expose myself to the difficulties.

Once we do that, we begin to find that in life we can avoid unnecessary suffering. It doesn't mean we avoid the underlying issues, but we do things in a way we can handle. We no longer crash into situations that are too big for us. This sort of understanding gives us a wonderfully flexible and intelligent way of working with ourselves in the world and with others. If, for example, we are working in business, we will very soon spot areas that our business associates can't handle. We may see how they precipitate themselves into their areas of difficulty. Then they become impossible, unreasonable, and irrational. So we help them. Very quietly, help them to not get into those areas. Then things work out much better. We do the same for ourselves.

This shows us that meditation is actually a highly practical activity because as we learn inwardly about all these things, we see the outward play. Inward and outward are always reflections of one another. So it can be a lot of fun after a while.

6

True Tranquillity

Without resisting or reacting

How to Catch a Monkey

When our mindfulness has strengthened to the point where we are present in the moment with the arising and passing of each thought and feeling, we will begin to gain insight into, and direct understanding of, our own grasping mechanisms. This is when we begin to understand what is meant by freedom from thought. We want to be free. At a certain level we know that we are in bondage. What we generally don't realize is that the bondage is of our own creation. There is a very good Indian story that illustrates this situation. It's about how to catch a monkey.

What you do if you want to catch a monkey is attach an empty calabash to the ground and cut a small hole in it, just big enough for the monkey to get his hand through when his fingers are extended. Inside you put some nuts. Monkey comes along, puts his hand through into the calabash and grabs a handful of nuts, and guess what. He can't get his hand out. So he is caught. You just stroll up and monkey screams and struggles and jumps around but he never thinks of letting go of his nuts. So you've got him. You've got him by the nuts.

And this is exactly us. We grasp, but can't see where. The place we are grasping is the idea of "me"—the egocentric fixation. We've got caught in compulsive cycles of thinking and we have fixated on the idea of a self. That is the fist closed around the nuts. As long as we are holding on to that self that we have made into something precious, our hand is trapped in the calabash. This is because we haven't realized the connection between that grasping and bondage.

So we start to understand the meaning of letting go. It's not just using this phrase and saying, "let go." Letting go is a very highly disciplined action. It is the action of training ourselves to see and know and be present with that moment of arising. Then to see the compulsive cycle of buying into the incoming thought through the three modes of grasping: grasping desire by trying to grab, grasping rejection by trying to push away, and grasping negation by trying to block it out. All three of these constitute grasping because every time we engage in one of these we get caught in whatever thought or feeling is there, because it is all reactive. Any reactive movement within the mind leads to bondage as it does in life.

The Reactivity of the Mind

If we are reactive in life, we are going to get into difficulties in our relationships. Many of our misunderstandings and problems arise because we are reactive. Why? Because reactivity not only triggers an immediate response but when there is a reactive quality in the mind, it's going to snag more emotional material than the moment demands. It won't respond to just that immediate situation, it will bring a whole lot of unresolved psychological baggage that is evoked by that immediate moment. So reactivity is almost invariably in excess of what is there. In meditation, we discover that reactive processes engage our habitual patterning. So we get stuck in a river of glue every time we react.

If we see this in our meditation, then—instead of identifying with the reactive tendency—we simply let it happen.

Imagine for example our favorite enemy insulting us in their favorite way. Perhaps we have a hangover and are tired so we just can't be bothered to respond. Suddenly the whole situation is different. A look of startled surprise comes over the person's face because the usual isn't happening. The good old fight hasn't taken place. It's quite disconcerting when that happens and for once we feel quite free.

With the mind this is far more powerful. At the first moment of not engaging thought or feeling a tremendous freedom arises in the mind. A feeling of relaxed spaciousness. There is no pushing thought and feelings away. They are there and can do what they like but we have just not engaged them.

Then we begin to understand that thoughts and feelings are like a river. Thoughts are arising within the mind, but they are arising within what we call the activity mind. It becomes clear, then, that the observer consciousness is the place from which the reactivity comes. It is also the place where the intelligence of insight and mindfulness enable us not to engage. We are able to let it go because we realize that we are not those thoughts.

The Buddha illustrated this point one day when he was giving a lecture and a Brahmin got up and began insulting him. He raved for while and when he had finished the Buddha said, "If somebody laid out a banquet in front of me, to whom would it belong?"

"Obviously it would belong to the person who put it there," replied the Brahmin.

"And if the person offered it to me," continued the Buddha, "and I declined to accept it, whose would it be?"

"Well, obviously it would remain the property of the person who put it there."

"Just so," declared the Buddha, "just so."

In our external relationships if people insult us and want to fight with us then that's their banquet. It becomes ours only if we choose to accept and engage it. It is exactly the same with all our thoughts and feelings. They are arising and passing but are problematic only because we pick them up. We make them ours, thus bringing a sense of egocentric possession to a situation that could have remained neutral. Only when the decision is made to appropriate the thought to ego-territory does grasping arise. When we don't do that then the mind relaxes, it is no longer caught up with all the thoughts and feelings and we understand what is meant by freedom. Freedom from thought.

The mind is now becoming more and more stable because it is no longer possible for the average change in thought/feeling to overwhelm that mind. The basis for the instability is no longer there. Once again the basis for instability is our compulsive conviction that whatever arises has to be experienced in the sense of being grasped in one of the three modes. We no longer have that belief. We've learnt that we no longer have to do that.

PRACTICE 8

Engaging Content

The mind is enslaved because it continually engages content, identifying with thoughts and feelings as they arise, and getting glued to them.

With the development of bare attention this will change and the compulsive reactive response that causes us to pick up on thought will weaken.

The main reason we engage is that the mind carries messages which say, "it is normal," "this is how I am," "I should do this." This attitude of mind constitutes an inner authority that dominates and sometimes tyrannizes our thinking. The result is we can't observe our thoughts objectively, but are compelled to get in and change, control, get rid of (especially unwanted feelings), and so on. The basic steps are:

- We identify with thought or feeling: "my thought," "my feeling." This makes it important because it then becomes "me," the basis of "my" identity.
- Having identified, we make it important: it matters, so I have to do something about it, own it and so on.

Until we understand this and challenge the underlying compulsive response, we remain in bondage.

The Practice

1. Meditate and observe the arising of thought/feeling.
2. In that moment, see how the mind engages.

3. See if you can spot the compulsive content which says "I must."
4. See how part of this is the definition of what is important—"It's important, that's why I must . . ."
5. Free yourself by the constant reminder—"It's not important. I don't have to . . ."

TIME: Do this for a few minutes at the end of a session for two weeks.

Tranquillity Is Not Fabricated

In the English language, *tranquillity* is a much misunderstood word because many of us want to be blissed out. When we meditate—or whatever we do—what we most want is to be comfortable. That's the bottom line. We're prepared to give up everything else provided we can be comfortable. Of course, the optimum is to be blissed out. But we are prepared to settle for the comfortable option if we can't manage bliss.

There is quite a combination of unseen factors at play here and most of us have them. Deep down we always want that optimum psychological state. This is why we have been looking at the problem of goals. Usually our idea of being blissed out is equated with not having any more thoughts. We believe that somehow, if we go the right route, we will find this switch in our heads that we can click and all thoughts will stop, all feelings will immediately change into bliss and that we can do it whenever we want to.

This attitude is a product of our mechanistic age. We do this in life as well. If we don't want the noise of the vacuum cleaner, we go and switch it off. If we don't want a headache, we take a pill. We believe that every dimension of our life should be amenable to this mechanical manipulation. We expect meditation to be the same. We think tranquillity is some form of bliss that we step into, leaving the whole world and all our psychological conditioning behind.

Tranquillity is not like that. It is something much better. It is a resilient state of mind that remains stable and has an open, spacious calm about it no matter what is going on within and around it. If our mind is experiencing tranquillity, thoughts and feelings can arise but they don't disturb us or throw us off balance. They are simply there. They arise, we observe them, they go. If there are painful thoughts, that's OK. The same with neutral and positive thoughts. They are all observed and experienced equally with the same stability. That's the tranquil mind.

If we understand this, then we won't expect our meditation to produce radical change or new mind states. What happens is that, slowly within our existing state of affairs, this new quality begins to emerge along with our mindfulness. We are slowly able to be present with more and more different conditions and not always be thrown by them into reactivity.

Tranquillity is not fabricated. We don't force it to happen. It's also not something precious and fragile. Tranquillity can remain in the midst of a great disaster provided the mind is continually open to all that's going on around it without resisting or reacting. It doesn't mean that we are now fireproof. We still have painful emotions. We can still be hurt, have fear and anxiety, but the difference is that those states are now experienced in a different way because we are not buying into them. So with tranquillity comes equanimity.

Many people believe that to meditate we have to remove ourselves from the normal activity of life and create special conditions so that we can be tranquil. Most people think that we have to go out into the countryside, sit by a beautiful pool, under a lovely tree, and so on. Although that may help, it's not necessary. We can cultivate tranquillity in the middle of a city if we know how to focus the mind in mindfulness.

Over and over again it comes back to the same thing. Mindfulness is the basis. If we train in mindfulness, tranquillity, awareness, equanimity, and insight arise. When we develop insight we see the grasping of thought and automatically let it go. Until we've seen the grasping, we don't let it go. We are the monkey caught in the calabash. If the monkey finally realized its fist was the problem, it would let go. This is why Krishnamurti said, "the seeing is the doing." When we see what is happening psychologically, that is what changes the mind. We don't then have to perform some manipulation.

Obstacles and Openness

I have talked quite a bit about habitual tendencies. In terms of negativity within the mind, these are the most important issues. They are very profound and deeply rooted. Unknown to us, at a conscious level, we are continually carried on the raft of habitual tendency.

Like the currents that carry a boat on the ocean, these habitual tendencies have been with us since we were born. Although quite a lot of our personality is molded through genetic inheritance, conditioning in life, and the way we are treated, all those influences are simply modifications of the tendencies we bring with us, our karmic tendencies.

If we understand this, we won't expect to bring about fast, radical change within the mind. This doesn't mean we can't change the mind at all, it just means we become more realistic. We come to terms with the fact that these negative states will arise because we have cultivated them over many lifetimes. We have put so much effort, for so long, into cultivating them that they are going to continue to arise for a long time. That is why acceptance is so important.

When we recognize them we are no longer deluded as to the state of our minds. Delusion is one of the major aspects of the mind. We are deluded because we think we are not what we are. So we identify the major habitual patterns. Then we make friends with them because these patterns are probably going to continue to arise throughout our lives. They will continue to be a major force in our lives and it is unreasonable to think that we can get rid of them. So we make friends with them and learn to work with them. We learn to be completely open, honest, and frank with ourselves, the way we are.

This is what makes some practitioners look a bit crazy. As they are really coming to terms with their negative mind states they are not necessarily acting them out—but nor are they pretending anymore that they are not like that. Just being very simple, with themselves and with others.

I remember being at a dinner party once where a guy revealed something about himself, which embarrassed a few people. Somebody had quite a strong reaction about this and voiced it. He just shrugged his shoulders and said, "That's me."

It's that sort of attitude. "I'm not going to pretend to you, or myself, that that's not there." That's the basis for very honest and skillful working with the mind.

This attitude is also illustrated in a lovely story of a yogi who was training in Tibet. He had got quite far with his training. He was living up in his cave and came down once every six months to visit his Lama and his sponsor who gave him a bag of *tsampa*, Tibetan porridge, twice a year. He was an interesting person because before he became a yogi he was a bandit. In Tibet, men didn't have many options for professions. Either you became a monk, a government official, a trader, a farmer and herder, or a thief. That was about the range available to the average person.

He had been a very successful bandit and decided that now he wanted to get enlightened instead. So he entered into his enlightenment training with the same verve and efficiency that he had applied to being a robber.

He was in the front parlor of his sponsor's house, who was a very rich merchant. In this room there were some beautiful objects around and at a certain point the sponsor was called out. Then he suddenly heard the yogi, who was now sitting by himself, shouting, "I've caught a thief! I've caught a thief!" The sponsor ran into the front room. There was nobody else there, but the yogi's hand was extended towards a very expensive vase and he had caught it with his other hand!

This sort of objectivity about ourselves is what arises when we train in mindfulness. We actually catch ourselves in the act. And it can become very humorous! This is where we learn the basis for working with obstacles, because they all arise out of negative karmic conditioning. So we train in fundamental acceptance and openness. This can be regarded as an adjunct to meditation because it trains us to adopt a new attitude towards ourselves and our lives.

A Spectrum of Practices

Another dimension of practice is purification. We need to purify the stream of our karmic conditioning. In my own practice, that of Vajrayana Buddhism, the first meditations are related to purification. Vajrayana or Tantra is a system of meditation and mind training that works directly to transform untapped, unconscious energies of the mind. Through visualization and relaxation, fragmented energies are purified of negative and conflicting tendencies. This leads to inner harmony and integration. The mind that has attained these states is able to embark upon the profound path of unfolding the deepest inner potentials of the mind. This path leads to the actualization of the highest human potential, called liberation or enlightenment in Buddhism. Vajrayana meditation methods are very powerful: they are designed to free meditators from every possible form of negativity and ego grasping. Vajrayana is often called "the Diamond Way," because a diamond cuts through all other substances.

We've been doing unskillful things for numerous lifetimes. We have done skillful things as well. It's because of the skillful things that we are able to be here and meditate at all. It's because of the harmful things that being here and meditating haven't made us enlightened in the first ten minutes. So now we begin the process of purifying the effects of our negative karma. This includes specific purifying meditations. These incorporate training in mindfulness, but they take one further. As soon as we engage our negativity in the Tantric practices, we feel changes because the practices change the negativity. That is the power of Vajrayana practice: it includes the stages of transforming and purifying negative emotionality and then strengthening and bringing into manifestation the enlightened qualities. They are extremely powerful practices. A lot of material is available on this topic and meditators can follow up for themselves.

Now we begin to get an idea of the range of meditation practices available to us. Not only training in mindfulness and developing tranquillity and insight, but also transformation and purification. These all mesh into one another.

But within all of these practices, the one fundamental essential is mindfulness. Without mindfulness it is almost impossible to do any of the others, because the mind is just too wayward. Just drifting away all the time, never present.

Q & A

Why would we stay alive after we are enlightened?
What did the Buddha do after he was enlightened?

He taught.
That's right. He helped other beings, millions if not billions of beings to enlightenment. So that's like asking, "What I don't understand is why you stay alive after you have got your medical degree." That's when you really start doing something useful!

Are all our actions always an expression of ego.
As long as you are not enlightened, yes. The Buddha was asked, towards the end of his life:

"What have you been doing for the last thirty or forty years?"

"Nothing," said the Buddha. "I haven't done a single thing."

"But you've spent all this time talking, teaching, and training people."

The Buddha: "I didn't do that because there was no sense of me as a self doing it. It was just spontaneous enlightened activity."

So everything we do as human beings who are unenlightened comes from an egocentric perspective. If our motivation and intention is good, then we can still help, but as long as the mind is locked in egocentric grasping, there is going to be an element of distortion. It comes from the assumption of self.

*We can see that history has repeated itself in terms of wars and
all the consequences of ego grasping. If tranquillity and liberation
are so powerful, why have they made such little impact on those
habitual patterns of the world? Why do so few people attempt to
attain enlightenment?*

There are many reasons for this. One reason, we are told,
is that we are living in a particularly perverse age at the
moment. What that means is that there is less interest in this
sort of thing than there has been in previous times. If you look
at the time of the Buddha, thousands, maybe even millions
of people were flocking to meditate and many became enlightened. But despite that, your observation is a very important one.

Let's look at our situation here and how difficult it is for us
to do what we are doing. First of all, human activity is normally
motivated by some form of gratification. We want rewards.
Almost everything we do is for a reward at the level of our five
senses. We get money, love, food, or we get drunk, or we get
stoned. We become more famous and powerful. So these are
done for sensory gratification. We are brought up with mas-
sively powerful assumptions that this is why we as humans do
things. What keeps us going in any direction is the continual
promise of reward. I'm willing to bet that generally the only reason we go to work is that we are rewarded with a paycheck at
the end of each month.

Now let's look at what happens when we meditate. In the
beginning there is no reward. Quite the contrary. We sit down,
do something so difficult that in the beginning we can't understand what we are supposed to be doing. Then we get sore
knees, a sore back; we get bored and tired. We get stiff, so it is
very unrewarding physically. It is unrewarding mentally because it is boring. Psychologically we might start encountering

the arising of negative mind states so there is no reward at that level.

There is no reward in terms of our reputation. Nobody congratulates us. And certainly nobody pays us to go and meditate. You don't get a check at the end of the month for meditating, it's quite the reverse! They say to you, "We need money." So you pay for it as well!

The more we look at it, the more we see that in terms of our normal activity none of our normal reward stimulus factors are present.

Another aspect of human mentality is that most of us opt for the quick fix. Particularly in this age. We are deeply conditioned to believe that there is a quick solution available for everything including the state of our mind. "That's what I want!"

If our quick fixes haven't worked in other areas, then we turn to meditation. We are definitely going to meditate for the quick fix. So we walk into our local meditation center and the first thing we hear is, "It's going to take you the rest of your life just to make a slight difference to your mind state." That's not the deal we want! We want somebody to say to us, "Do my technique for ten minutes, pay me a hundred dollars, and I guarantee you will walk out of here feeling great." That's what we want!

Unfortunately, that's not what is on offer. So people don't want to make the effort. It does require sustained effort.

There is also an even more interesting dimension. We can't see very good examples of people who have meditated because there are not that many around in our materialistic society. But when people do see the examples of accomplished meditators, the qualities they are manifesting are almost impossible to recognize unless we have developed a little bit of understanding ourselves. There are very few role models to inspire us and give us confidence that we can actually do it.

7

The Path
Is Obstacles

But, everything is workable

Obstacles arise via our conditioned reflexes. These are rooted in the fundamental negative mind states that the Buddha called the mind poisons of greed, hatred, delusion, pride, and jealousy. This provides the basis for our habitual tendencies so that negative states naturally arise within the mind until they have been purified. These arise in the form of obstacles and are very often not seen for what they are.

They arise within our familiar territory and have the authority of familiarity. Obstacles, for example, may arise in the form of a changed mood. We sit down to meditate and think, "This is great, I'm going to meditate." After about ten minutes our knees hurt, we're bored. The obstacle arises in the form of a changed mood. We don't feel like meditating any more. "It's pointless to meditate if I don't feel like meditating. I'm wasting my time. I'd be much better employed if I went and made a cup of tea, I think that's what I'll do." So off we go.

We have been carried out of the room quite authentically because we now "knew" that there was no point in carrying on with meditation because we didn't feel like it any more. And if we don't feel like it, it's a waste of time. We know that, it's a fact to us. That is why we are not enlightened: because we have always followed that factual route, which is paved with lies. We are buying into obstacles. There are thousands of these.

Then there are bigger ones and these are much juicier. We're meditating and we start to realize that we are very neurotic. We have an obsessive-compulsive neurotic state that causes us always to feel sorry for ourselves. So instead of meditating, we spend our session reviewing the problems our lives have presented to us. All the misfortunes and reasons why other people are happy and we're not. Whatever our cycle is.

By the end of the session we have convinced ourselves that meditation doesn't work. What we really need is to go to California and have a whole lot of primal screams! Something quite drastic and radical. Then again we believe we need psychiatric treatment. Perhaps we should go and do therapy instead of meditation. There may be an element of truth in that but it doesn't mean we don't continue with our meditation. It just means we are recognizing a different dimension.

Meditation is not just calm sailing. It can sometimes be a stormy sea. It also has the hidden reefs that we have talked about: assumptions, expectations, goals, and so on. We need to let go of the naïve view, that if we sit and meditate everything is going to become peaceful and wonderful. When we meditate, obstacles are going to arise. But, everything is workable. We train ourselves to work with obstacles.

One of the greatest strengths of Vajrayana is that it is designed to work with obstacles. It works on the understanding that the path is obstacles. This is why we are trained to bring all conditions to the path. We turn everything into the path of liberation. The bigger the obstacle, the bigger the opportunity because a great deal of energy is contained in that obstacle. It's like a huge dung heap. If you have a lot of dung you are going to be able to grow beautiful vegetables. If you just have an open, barren piece of ground, you are not going to grow much. After a while, the true practitioner welcomes obstacles.

Near Enemies

Near enemies are the sorts of mind states we dwell in most of the time—substitutes for the real thing, almost but not quite there, which arise when the mind grasps pure, spontaneous feelings and causes them to manifest as something disturbing instead of liberating. Where there is pure mindfulness and freedom from grasping, we experience the arising of a range of pure emotional states. The easiest one to understand is joy. Joy is a very light, vivid, sparkling experience that comes into the mind that relates to something internal or external without grasping.

For example, we get up one morning and look out the window at a beautiful sunrise. The common experience within a human mind is to experience joy in relation to that sunrise. That joy arises from a level of consciousness which is not involved with egocentric grasping. So it is experience without an experiencer. It usually lasts for only a fraction of an instant. That is a pure state.

Within an instant, however, consciousness has conducted its surveillance, recognized, evaluated, decided that this is what it wants, and then grasped. That is the moment when joy is lost: the moment the egocentric sense appropriates joy. Then there is no joy left. What we have instead is the near enemy, which is excitement. Joy is the pure state because it lacks grasping. Excitement is the near enemy because it arises when the mind destroys joy by grasping it.

This is what we are doing continuously in life. There is a moment of pure love. Then it is appropriated and it becomes possessive love. My love. My object. We can see this very often in a relationship. Two people meet and get on really well. There is then a short period, depending on the level of their grasping, where there may be a joyful experience of one another's company. But after a while that condition is subverted and it becomes territorial: my partner. That is near enemy. There is no more joy left. It is then a constant maneuvering of possessiveness.

When we train in mindfulness and understand observer consciousness and activity mind, what begins to happen is we lose the sense of an observer. There is just a process of observing without the sense of a being who observes. When mindfulness is stable we will start freeing ourselves from the near enemies because we will see the grasping arising.

PRACTICE 9
The Three Modes

The untrained mind always grasps at thoughts in one of three ways:

- Attachment—holding onto what it likes.
- Negation—trying to block out whatever doesn't interest it.
- Rejection—fighting to "get rid of" what it does not like.

These three modes are the causes of attachment and turmoil

in the mind. When we gradually learn to identify and let go of them, the mind settles into a deeper level of stability. It approaches equanimity.

The Practice

Meditate.

Every now and again, when you find yourself drawn into distraction, step back and look at the thought.

Which of the three modes is it manifesting?

TIME: Do this for one or two sessions once a week for a year.

8

Enlightenment

Nowhere to go, nothing new to create

A Diamond Buried in Mud

Writers have tried to describe enlightenment. Usually it is described in terms of the qualities that arise in the mind and of the states that fall away. This is the best we can do.

Enlightenment is when all the inherent enlightened qualities manifest and when all the obscurations which prevent our experience of them fall away. So it is not a goal that we can strive for. The very act of striving will keep us trapped within the cycle of thinking. Enlightenment is already there—like a diamond buried in mud. It is not something we have to go and find and bring home. It is already there. Which is why, in our meditation, in the very beginning, we train ourselves in knowing that we have nothing to strive for. Nowhere to go, nothing new to create. It's all here already. The path of training is simply systematically to remove the obstacles. To free ourselves from the mind poisons. The route to that, inevitably, is mindfulness.

In some schools of Buddhism it is said that enlightenment is not possible except in the time of a Buddha. To me, that is a misunderstanding of the Buddha's teaching. Others say enlightenment is not possible now because we are in a dark age. It seems to me that is also a misunderstanding and a perversion of the Buddha's teaching. Nowhere have I read the Buddha saying that that is the case.

If you look at Buddhism within the context of Vajrayana, Tibetan Buddhism, Lamas are quite unequivocal: "Enlightenment is possible in a lifetime." If we really look at that statement, it frees us from the ambitious mentality that says, "I must accumulate credentials." What it is pointing to is that the human mind can, at any moment, experience enlightenment once it has truly understood letting go. So it is also emphasizing that the good boy or girl isn't necessarily going to become enlightened before the bad boy. If I'm a goodie-goodie and think I'm nearer enlightenment than you are, I'm probably further away. Even though I might be good and living a very noble and moral life, I might be so caught up in my self-congratulatory pride that that stops me becoming enlightened.

It is important to let go of this sort of thinking because often we think we are particularly bad or useless. We rejoice in these sorts of mind states where we have preciously nurtured a sense of guilt, inadequacy, failure, hopelessness. We nurture them and constantly feed them. We use them as a way of not enabling ourselves to break free and not experience our potential. This point is illustrated to some degree in the humorous story of the Buddha and two monks.

The Buddha was walking along one day and these two monks spotted him. So they trotted up because they had been having a debate about enlightenment. One monk asked, "When will I become enlightened, how many lifetimes?"

"For you, seven lifetimes," said the Buddha.

This monk was over the moon. He thought it was fantastic and he went off really happy.

"And how many lifetimes for me?" asked the second monk.

"Do you see that tree over there?" said the Buddha pointing to a large tree with hundreds of thousands of leaves on it. "For you, as many lifetimes as there are leaves on that tree."

The monk looked at the tree and lost all hope. At that moment he became enlightened.

Unfortunately, it seems that enlightenment is possible. We have no excuses. That doesn't mean we beat ourselves to death trying to get enlightened just because somebody said enlightenment was possible in a lifetime. But it can release us from what could otherwise be a sense of hopelessness which turns our practice into a mere formality. That is what happens when people really lose the essence of what it is about. Their practice becomes formal and lifeless. In Vajrayana, the focus is on doing it for others. So we really buy into this motivation of knowing that we can help others. No matter how inadequate we feel, it is possible for us to change our minds so that we can become a beneficial force in the world. More than that, we can start the process going of creating the karmic causes and conditions for our eventual enlightenment, even if it is not in this lifetime.

When we reflect in this way, we get a much more workable, long-term perspective about our lives. Perhaps at the moment our lives are all about obstacles, weaknesses, and difficulties but we start gaining a certain confidence that we are doing what is necessary.

When we combine this attitude with *bodhisattva** motiva-

---

* A bodhisattva is one who sets out to become enlightened for the benefit of others, and lives purely to benefit sentient beings.

tion, we then have the fundamental motivation to be able to practice and become enlightened. The essence of whether we practice or not is motivation. If we haven't grounded our motivation, our practice will falter and peter out. If we have grounded our motivation, if we really know why we are practicing, then we will keep at it.

Regular practice is the most important thing for busy people. Creating a program, and sticking to it. Practice every day. The other aspect of regular practice is the meditation center. Most of us need help in a whole variety of ways. One of those ways is just the encouragement of knowing that other people are doing the same thing. That is why we have group practices at centers. If we get involved in these, we find that they keep us going—the fact that we know there are others doing it.

If we have our motivation in place, then we support it. Support it with what is offered. Take advantage of it. It's not useful to set about it with the sense that we are doing somebody else a favor. We are not doing anyone a favor by sitting and meditating every morning. We are just helping ourselves. But in the long term, through that, we will be able to help others. So work that one through and get a practical approach to it.

The image of the diamond is used in Vajrayana Buddhism. Its sparkling purity is suggestive of the ever-present enlightened mind which is within each one of us.

It goes further. The diamond is the hardest of gems, and manifests an adamantine quality. Its power severs all obstacles—nothing can withstand its sharp strength. For us this is the most encouraging news—although our diamond minds may seem to be enmeshed in a tangle of obscurations, we will surely cut free!

Appendix

Guidelines for Helpers

Practices 1 and 2: Meditation Using a Support

Ensure the group understands that the support is not a point of concentration, but a support upon which the mind rests to help it remain in focus. Essentials:

- Soft, relaxed attention
- No wrenching back, striving, or rigidity
- No blocking or suppression of thoughts or feelings
- Never trying to get rid of thoughts or feelings
- Allowing the mind to throw up its usual patterns of thinking or feeling without blocking, but equally without engaging and following—without becoming involved and developing thoughts

After each session ask the meditators for feedback to ensure they are not falling into these traps. It takes time to learn to work skillfully with the support. Help meditators use these practices to understand the perversity of the mind, as well as the following points.

Practice 1: When thought is made the focus, the mind often plays tricks—like refusing to continue with the thought. So we learn to understand the insubstantial nature of thought and become content to remain with the support. It is easier then to allow thoughts to flow by.

Practice 2: A relaxed, open mind is being developed here. This is essential for meditation. Meditation is not an act of doing or tackling a task. It is learning to rest the mind in mindfulness which is a state. It is non-active. Meditation is a state, not an activity.

Repeat the practices three or four times, until you feel meditators are beginning to understand how to rest their minds in an open, receptive way instead of striving to achieve something.

Practice 3: Observer Consciousness and Activity Mind

This practice has three purposes:

1. To help the meditator understand the multi-dimensional nature of mind, beginning with observer and observed.
2. To show that somewhere in the mind is an idea of a self. That idea resides in the observer consciousness, and considers itself to be the thinker, until this exercise reveals otherwise.
3. To reveal to the meditator that observing and thinking are two separate processes. When this is realized an important understanding dawns: "I am not these thoughts." The meditator identifies with the thoughts, gives them energy

and seems to become them, but is manifestly not them because they arise independently of the observer and can thus be observed.

Although the practice is very simple, it is profound because it lays the foundation for freedom—freedom from thought, and finally freedom from the idea of a thinker.

Do you see that?

Let meditators practice for five or ten minutes then ask for feedback. Ask questions such as: Who was thinking? Where did thoughts come from? Which of the two parts of the mind is "me"? Help them challenge the assumption that thinker and thought are the same. Use the analogy of the five senses: The observer mind sees visual objects with the eye—does it become the object? It hears with the ear—does it become the sound?

Emphasize to the group that because thoughts arise inwardly we assume we are them. But this is no more the case than with sights, sounds, smells, and the like.

Practice 4: Where Does My Mind Go?

Do this with the group after you have instructed them. Emphasize over and over again that they should do it in a very casual, relaxed way. It's not a big deal. No getting it right or wrong. It's just observing what is constantly happening. No need to strive and strain to work out categories. Let them reveal themselves.

After the twenty-minute session—with ten minutes maximum on the main part of the exercise—ask how they got on. Get them to tell you where their minds went. Help them see it as a fun exercise—not a test or threat. Help them develop an attitude of being able to observe their mind activity with a degree of humor and objectivity.

The usual categories of distraction are:

- Thinking about the past—just generally mulling over memories
- Re-working the past—analyzing past events, rerunning old fights, arguments, situations
- Commenting on and analyzing present mind activity; analytical, present moment surveillance
- Future planning or just thinking about the future generally
- Fantasizing/daydreaming. This sometimes has a time slot. It may be just escapist or substitution fantasy
- Combinations of these

Get the group to add their own. Help them accept the fact that the mind always does these things. In discussion, see if they can identify the underlying emotional condition that fuels the mind's need to take off on its particular route.

Practice 5: Backtracking

Some meditators have difficulty with this in the beginning because they are unable to recall the links or steps. Encourage them to keep at it—they will soon overcome the problem.

Another difficulty is that they begin backtracking but very soon get carried away by a new line of thinking and so are never able to retrace more than a few steps. This again will change with perseverance.

A few rounds of this practice will increase clarity and understanding about the process of thinking.

Practice 6: The Moment of Arising

Thoughts arise from many sources, in association with

- physical sensation
- sound
- smell
- a preceding thought that was still hovering when attention was returned to the support
- memory

Some thoughts simply erupt into the mind without any apparent preceding associative event.

This game is the basis for the meditator being able to see and understand "freedom from thought." Great clarity at the moment of arising reveals all the subliminal processes that happen here.

This concludes an interconnected triad:

- Where does my mind go?
- Backtracking
- Moment of arising

Practice 7: The Cycle of Thought

Sometimes the stages are more easily seen in retrospect, so if someone is having difficulty observing during meditation, spend time at the end of a session looking back. It's easiest to begin with the fact that the thought is there and then work backwards and forwards to see arising and passing.

A useful aid is to focus on sound and see how sounds follow the same cycle. If you are meditating near a road you can observe how the sound of a car follows the cycle. If there are many cars it is difficult to sort out the cycle of one specifically because of the jumble of noise. The mind is the same—if there are many thoughts there seems to be an impenetrable tangle.

It helps to know how some thoughts pass:

- Overtaken and replaced by another thought
- Mind simply drifts out of focus and loses track of it
- Meditator returns to support and thought falls away
- Falls asleep and loses contact
- Mind is jolted into another focus by a sound, smell, etc.
- If energy is not fed into the thought it will simply die away

The value of this practice is that one learns that thoughts really are insubstantial and have no solid "entity-ness." As the Buddha said, "This too will pass." This understanding transforms suffering and frees the mind.

Practice 8: Engaging Content

This is one of the most difficult practices because it depends upon a fair degree of mindfulness and insight. Help meditators spot the underlying "authority" component by asking them why they keep following thoughts even when they are boring or meaningless.

Practice 9: The Three Modes

Help the group understand that equanimity arises slowly and is experienced in meditation as "one taste." All thoughts are just thoughts. The mature meditator passes beyond good, bad, and indifferent. This takes time to understand.

Acknowledgments

We wish to thank the many people who have made the publication of this book possible:

Lama Yeshe Losal for his foreword and blessing;
Louis Baum for highly professional advice and guidance;
Karel Shoeman for insightful criticism;
Joseph Goldstein and Sister Ellen Finlay for their confidence and encouragement–even though they are on the other side of the world;
Brad Hammond for concepts and transcriptions;
Kobus Geldenhuys for his bright ideas and Achim von Arnim for the sparkling title;
Mark Borchers for the concept of "exploring consciousness";
Beryl Schutten for some final polishing;
Mel Cohen, Mike Kantey, Karin Cronjé;
All the meditators and friends;
And our guardian angel without whom there would have been no Kairon Press: Joe van Dorsten.

For this edition, we would like to thank Samuel Bercholz, Peter Turner, Jonathan Green, Joel Segel, and all at Shambhala Publications for their support.

Rob Nairn and Erika van Greunen
Kairon Press, Kalk Bay

About the Author

Rob Nairn was born and educated in Zimbabwe. While training in law, psychology, and criminology, he pursued his interest in religion and meditation. In 1964 he began training under meditation masters in India, and was instructed by His Holiness the Dalai Lama to return to Africa and teach. In the following years he spent all his spare time in retreats and under the guidance of lamas and other meditation teachers, including Thrangu Rinpoche, Akong Rinpoche, Dhiravamsa, and Joseph Goldstein.

In 1980 he was told by His Holiness the Sixteenth Gyalwa Karmapa, head of the Kagyu lineage, to teach Insight meditation. He resigned as professor of criminology at the University of Cape Town, and set up a retreat center at Nieu Bethesda in the Karoo in South Africa.

In 1989 Rob entered a traditional four-year retreat under the guidance of lamas at Samye Ling Tibetan Centre in Scotland. In isolation from the world he studied and practiced ancient methods of meditation that have brought many Tantric masters to enlightenment. In 1993 Dr. Akong Rinpoche, then Abbot of Samye Ling, sent Rob to head the Kagyu Centres in Africa.

Rob is a much sought-after lecturer on Buddhism and meditation at several Southern African universities, as well as in England, Scotland, Ireland, and the United States. His understanding of modern psychology, especially that of Carl Jung, enables him to translate ancient Eastern wisdom into terminology accessible to Westerners.